Nostalgic Coventry

Part of the
Memories
series

The Publishers would like to thank the following companies for supporting the production of this book

Main Sponsor

Lee Beesley

Charles Ager Limited

Neil Bartlett (Haulage) Limited

Belgrade Theatre Trust (Coventry) Ltd

Capitol Tile Supplies Limited

Coventry Building Society

Mike De Courcey Travel Limited

Deeley Group Limited

Exhall Plating Limited

Jaguar Cars

Park Sheet Metal Company Limited

H E Phillips Limited

PMD Group Limited

J & J Reason & Sons

Seymours - Solicitors

Shipley Europe Limited

Touchstone Housing Association Limited

First published in Great Britain by True North Books Limited
Units 3 - 5 Heathfield Industrial Park
Elland West Yorkshire
HX5 9AE
Tel. 01422 377977
© Copyright: True North Books Limited 1999

ISBN 1 900463 58 x

Text, design and origination by True North Books Limited, Elland, West Yorkshire
Printed and bound by The Amadeus Press Limited, Huddersfield, West Yorkshire

Memories are made of this

Memories. We all have them; some good, some bad, but our memories of the city we grew up in are usually tucked away in a very special place in our minds. The best are usually connected with our childhood and youth, when we longed to be grown up and paid no attention to adults who told us to enjoy being young, as these were the best years of our lives. We look back now and realise that they were right.

So many memories. And so many changes; one-way traffic systems, pedestrianisation, self-service shopping. New trends in shopping led to the very first self-serve stores being opened. How strange it felt at first to pick up a basket (those were the days before shopping trolleys!) and help ourselves from the goods on display on the shelves - it was almost like stealing! The trend led eventually to out-of-city shopping in centres.

Through the bad times and the good, however, Coventry not only survived but prospered. We have only to compare the city as it is today with its new shopping centres and up-to-the-minute facilities with the city as it was before the war to see what progress has been realised and what achievements have been made over the last 50 years.Coventry has a history to be proud of - but more importantly, a great future to look forward to, into the new millennium and beyond.

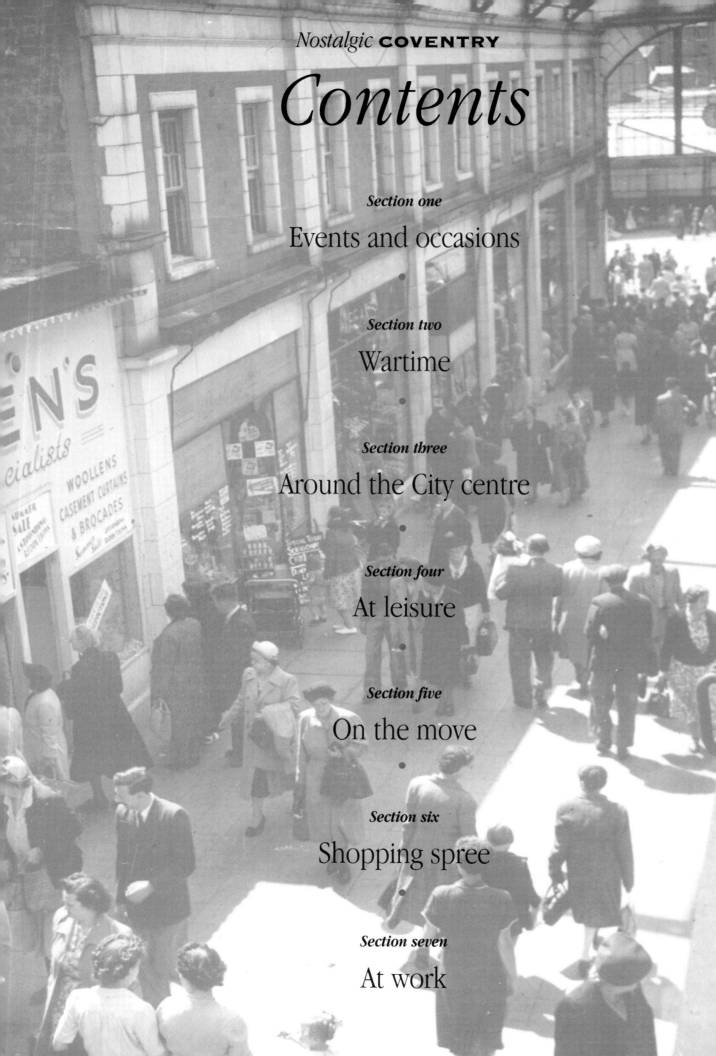

Nostalgic **COVENTRY**

Contents

Events & occasions

The end of the Great War of 1914-18 is approaching. The war to end all wars did no such thing. It provided the 20th century with one of its worst horrors and did little to satisfy the warmongers who coveted the territories of others. Yet, the ordinary man and woman in the street could only be immensely proud of those who had made such huge sacrifices in the name of king and country. They crowded the streets to show solidarity and support. It is not the clanking of trams that was heard on this day on Broadgate. The noise came from the steel monster rolling along its own tracks. It is 'tank bank' week. Money is being raised to fund the munitions factories and workers' housing. Less than two years

before, the tank had first been used in battle on the Somme. To maintain secrecy, the first ones had been shipped to the front in crates marked 'tanks'. The name stuck. Six months before this procession on Broadgate, 400 British tanks had broken through German lines at Cambrai. Eight thousand enemy troops and 100 field guns were captured. It was good propaganda to use the success of the tank to drum up further support for the war effort. Other towns and cities also held 'tank weeks' during 1918. Funds were raised to go towards building more aircraft, howitzers etc. Even in the Second World War similar schemes were thought up. These included an 'adopt a warship' sort of venture.

Above: Remember the James Bond films that featured the Carnival in Rio and the Mardi Gras in New Orleans? What about the Notting Hill Carnival? These have nothing on the ones in Coventry. (Well, we can all fantasise a little!) To the crowds thronging the pavements on the corner of Smithford Street and Broadgate in 1928, those faraway places meant very little. The bunting was flown, banners waved and happy faces turned towards the float. The carnival queen's chariot glided as serenely as the swan it was wrapped in. The liveried footmen pulling the centre-piece gave an added pomp to the pageantry of the day. The procession would have bands playing and acrobats tumbling. A fair would top off the festivities at the end of the day. But, for now, all eyes were upon Marjorie Biddulph as she rode proudly flanked by her Maids of Honour. Madge Collingbourne, Edith Varley and the Lucys, Page and Swain, were those so honoured on that day. Was there, though, a touch of envy hiding within their pride? 'Wouldn't I have made a prettier queen?' might have been an unspoken thought. Who could have blamed them if it were so? What a privilege to have been selected to represent the essence of Coventry. Mum and dad could dine out for 12 months on the reflected glory. In years to come, Marjorie could remind future generations that they weren't in the same class as her when it came to queening it!

What wonderful Christian names those young women had. They were just right for the time. Do you suppose that Kayleigh, Kylie or Kirsty will mean the same to our grand-children 70 years from now?

Above right: This is the end of the beginning. The first stage of the rebirth has been completed. The centre green of Broadgate witnesses the first of many unveiling ceremonies that are to come. Out with the old and in with the new. The reborn centre echoes to the happy sound of excited voices that welcome the young Princess Elizabeth. She has come to

perform the official opening ceremony of the new Broadgate. Any royal visit was an occasion of great interest. Bunting would fly from buildings and flags would wave a hello to whichever members of the family had graced the city with their presence. Of course, there weren't many structures around from which to hang those gaily coloured strips of cloth. That part of the redevelopment was years away from completion. It's now 1948. Only a few months ago the public had rejoiced in the princess's marriage to Prince Philip. Now she was here, sharing Coventry's joy. It seemed right that a youthful 22 year old should perform the ceremony. The future belonged to the young and it was the young who were our future. They had inherited a world torn apart by conflict. It would now be up to them to find a lasting peace and make it work. All eyes were on the woman who was to be head of state one day. Few watching could have guessed that the time was only four years further ahead. An even more poignant event was to lie in wait. Before the year was out, Princess Elizabeth would give birth to her first child, Charles.

The flag hanging from the window could have been unfurled on many an important occasion over the years. In 1948, it was flying to celebrate the reopening of Broadgate. In 1947, it had flown for the wedding of Princess Elizabeth. Two years before that, it had been at the centre of the rejoicing that surrounded VE and VJ days. Perhaps the self-same symbol of national pride had fluttered over the balcony at the coronation of George VI and at the jubilee of his father, the year before that. Possibly, the flag would last to welcome the arrival of the new baby royals, Charles and Anne, and the crowning of their mother in 1953. Flying the flag is a phrase that has passed into our vocabulary. Meaning to show pride in our national heritage, it could just as easily apply to the pride in our city that we all felt that day. Like a phoenix from the ashes, the rise was beginning. It wasn't only the bricks and mortar that would take shape and grow. The people's spirits were on the way up. Hand in hand, the changing scene that was Coventry and the people who were its life would soar above the problems that had come their way. As the second half of the century approached, the city knew this was the opportunity for renewal. Not in the obvious way of buildings, but in hearts and souls, with a determination to put the past behind and create a fabulous future. What had been sacrificed was not going to be in vain. In time, we would forgive. But, we would not forget.

The Godiva pageant was an important occasion for the locals. They turned up to line the streets in their thousands to witness the parade. The link with the historical legend of the lady with the flowing locks was to be celebrated as part of Coventry's heritage. If you wanted to cheer and risk throwing your hat in the air, a solution was on hand. Dunn & Co could provide a replacement for the one that failed to return from its orbit. The shop proudly claimed itself to be at the forefront of the cap and hat-making trade. It wasn't around in the 11th century when Lady Godiva made her famous ride. Anyway, she'd have needed more than a cap to cover her blushes! The float in this scene from 1929 was called 'Episode XV - Edward III'. It was one of many telling the history of the city. The tableau in the picture shows the official incorporation of Coventry being received by Nicholas Mitchell. This happened in 1345 when it was already one of the country's largest towns. King Edward's mother, Isabella, continued the royal connections. She made a gift of land to the Guild of St John the Baptist. St John's Church on Fleet Street was built there. Spectators may not have known the historical ins and outs - it was enough to have a family day out and enjoy the festivities. It was a time of depression in the job market,and any chance to have a bit of fun was to be treasured. If it could be mixed with acknowledging the past, then so much the better.

YOU COULD HEAR
THE CHEERING IN
KENILWORTH
WHEN PRINCESS
ELIZABETH
DEDICATED THE
NEW BROADGATE
IN 1948

The temporary grandstand was reserved for local bigwigs and officials. Out of picture was the life-blood of the city, its people. They had come in hordes to witness the opening of the new Broadgate. It was to them that Princess Elizabeth was talking. Her clipped speech was accepted as part of her class. Those who had come, that day in 1948, didn't mind the way she sounded. It was what she stood for that was important. Here, in front of us, was the heir to the throne. She was even carrying the next in line. Not all of us would have known that, but many of the women in our midst gave knowing looks. 'I think she is, you know.' Britain's future was guaranteed in the line of succession of the Windsor family. Not for us the republics of much of the rest of Europe. We had our monarchy and long may it continue. As the Princess read from her notes, the crowds listened respectfully to the dedication of Broadgate. When she finished, a great swell of noise swept over the crowd. They said you could hear the cheering in Kenilworth. 'God save the king' was sung with gusto. A few years later and it would be the Queen for whom our voices would be raised. Back in 1948 we didn't know that. We were just happy that she had come to share the day with us.

Below: The shops, which had been put up as temporary retail outlets, stand behind the other temporary structure, the grandstand. For once, they are not the centre of interest. Broadgate is ringed with people keen to see and listen to the words of the heir to the throne on her visit to perform the official opening ceremony of the new Broadgate. Even those who get only the smallest glimpse of her can say, 'I was there that day.' People at the front had stood patiently for hours in order to get the best spot. There was much crossing of legs. No chance of going to answer a call of nature. It would have been a nonsense to abandon a prime position, because, once surrendered, it wasn't going to be given back! The members of the St John's Ambulance Service were kept busy. Packed like sardines, there were quite a few fainting fits. Children would be passed over the heads of the crowd and the magic of the smelling salts, or a sip of water, would do the trick. Often the butt of cruel jibes, usually referring to their special place at important gatherings and sports matches, these volunteers did a fine job. At any large event, the black uniforms, with their distinctive white sashes, were always on hand. Their first aid training held them in good stead when dealing with the cuts, bruises and swooning fits that often came their way. The hours of practice put in meant that there was a skill on hand when faced with more serious situations. Broken bones could be splinted and artificial respiration administered.

> **PEOPLE STOOD FOR HOURS TO GET THE BEST SPOT FOR A VIEW OF PRINCESS ELIZABETH**

The St John's Service was often first to have to react in a major incident. There wouldn't be one of those today. Anyway, sshhh! The Princess is about to speak and we are all ears.

The nurses, like little sisters of mercy, move around the crowds, in case their talents are needed. Respect for them and their work was on a level with that given to nuns. Nursing had often been carried out by these saintly souls, caring for the sick and poor in the city slums, as well as in their own convents. There was almost a sort of religious similarity about their uniforms and headgear. That helped make nurses subject to our high regard. We placed them on the same pedestal. Just imagine the pride in being of personal service to Princess Elizabeth. What a privilege. That would have been something to talk about on the wards the following week. Ideas like that were just a flight of fancy, for now came the time to concentrate on the words being spoken from the platform. Afterwards, there might be work for those followers of the Florence Nightingale tradition. In amongst the crowd there were bound to be a few feeling the effects of the crush. Police and armed forces worked hard in keeping order, but the joy of the day would lead to careless accidents. Then, there would be a chance to put into practice all the training hours spent at nursing college. By tomorrow, it would be back to the mixture of pills and potions, bandages and bedpans. For now, let's scurry to get a good view.

Above: The Godiva pageant winds along the streets. The crowds stand to marvel at the hard work and planning that has gone into the event, once more. It reminded everyone of important milestones in Coventry's history. As well as that, the important industries of the city would be celebrated. Watch and clock making had, for about a century, been an important part of the economy in these parts. Outsiders can only think of Coventry and its place in motor and aero engine manufacture. This display, simply titled 'Tableau II', shows that precision engineering went further. Rotherham & Son, makers of fine timepieces, sponsored the float.

There was something else to cheer for on that day in 1951. The Union flags give the game away. It's the year of the Festival of Britain. Emerging from the gloom of the war years, it was good to see people giving themselves a pat on the back. There was much to acknowledge. Randolph Turpin would win the world middleweight boxing title and Max Faulkner the Open golf championship. Even old Winnie was on his way back to number ten. The corner had been turned and the decade ahead would bring the better days that the free world had fought for. The festival was to coincide with the centenary of the Victorians' Great Exhibition. The Royal Festival Hall and Pleasure Gardens were built in London. Some weren't so keen about the cost and called the programme 'Morrison's Folly'. Not much changes. Look at the controversy over 'Mandelson's Madness' - the Millennium Dome.

Below: It looks busy enough, now. Wait another hour or two and there will be just a sea of heads ranging across Broadgate. Necks craning for a better view, a sense of expectancy will fall on the crowd.

A great day is coming and we will be there to share it. The lucky ones have had the sense to come early. The best spots are being bagged. Those who leave it to the last minute will be surprised. They will find that they are well back from the ropes and line of marshals. Even those of us who had the foresight to get here first need good eyes to get a decent look. Serve the others right, we planned ahead.

Waiting for the opening ceremony to begin, it was difficult to imagine how the centre would develop over the next decade. Exhibitions of the various plans were held. Models of the proposed revamping of the city were on display. The local paper had even sponsored competitions for its readers to have a say and submit their ideas. There were great problems in trying to balance the wishes of the traditionalist and the revolutionary. By 1957, Arthur Ling, the designer who replaced Donald Gibson, realised his plans for what are now the Smithford and Market Ways, which cut across the precinct. It was only then that Ministry approval had been granted for plans submitted in 1951. During that time, it had been envisaged that some 400,000 might, in stages, move from Birmingham to Coventry.

Left: Princess Margaret came for an official visit in 1957. She had come to honour a service of dedication at the new church in Tile Hill. Although a new satellite town, it didn't count as a garden city. To be classed as such, there had to be industry within it. Tile Hill wasn't given the status gained by Letchworth, the first of these created as long ago as 1903. The ins and outs of this didn't seem to worry locals who were jam-packed into every vantage point they could find in Coventry's precinct. Accompanied by the mayor, the Queen's sister could not be anything but impressed with the turn out. The walk-ways of the precinct creaked under the weight of the many who were keen to welcome her to their city. Princess Margaret was well known to the crowd. A popular figure in the gossip columns, her romance with Group Captain Peter Townsend had kept everyone enter-tained during 1955. When, under pres-sure from the church and government, it was called off, the nation thought 'Here we go again.' Less than 20 years before, her uncle had to give up the throne in similar circumstances. The royals have had the ups and downs of their love lives put under the micro-scope during most of the 20th century. Margaret Rose was just one in a long line. How the girls in the crowd would have bonded with her. They had dad telling them that such and such a lad was no good for them. The woman in front of them, that day, had politicians and bishops against her!

Above: The successful days of the smaller shop or store were to face many threats from the attractions of bigger rivals. In the 1980s, supermarkets started to sell more than just food on a wide scale. The growth of out of town hypermarkets and dedicated shopping centres threatened the little retailer even more. Such competition dated back to before the war. Then, it was the coming of the large department store that gave many a sleepless night to the owners of one or two room premises. In 1937 it was Owen & Owen who opened the furniture and department store which gave alarm to some and greater variety to others. It was to suffer bomb damage three years later. Alders is now its replacement.

The crowds had come to see both the new store and the opening of Trinity Street. Coventry has undergone a number of rebuilding programmes. It wasn't just the wartime destruction that caused new work to be commenced. Between the wars there were many houses and shops in need of renewal. They were run down and had long outlived their usefulness. Many were in a poor state of repair and quite a number of people lived in insanitary conditions. There was a new-found wealth from its booming motor and aircraft industries. The city needed to expand to allow more growth. It was in response to this that thousands turned out. They listened to the speeches relayed through the loudspeakers and shared mutual pride in Coventry's

Wartime

Below: These aren't the Ovaltinies. No happy smiling faces for us this day. What was there to chuckle about? Hitler had sent his planes to pour death and destruction out of the skies onto the unsuspecting homes of Coventry families. There had been some warnings in the time leading up to the major raid of November 1940. The airfield at Ansty had been bombed in June. The Rootes factory at Ryton had been hit by incendiaries and the Rex cinema on Corporation Street wrecked in August. Generally, damage was limited. Even the attack on the Standard factory at Canley was made by a single bomber. It was no surprise that these families were unready for the onslaught that had just come their way. Whatever they could salvage from their wrecked homes was hastily collected in carrier bags. Even prams could be used to ferry the few possessions that remained intact. Just in case the bombers returned, the lad on the left has his tin hat clamped to his head. He's not going to be caught napping next time. But, in times like these, the voluntary services showed their worth. With true British grit, the mobile canteens were on the streets within hours. A mug of hot soup or a cup of steaming tea could provide some inner warmth on this chilly autumn day. Then it would be off to start over again. Shocked we might have been, but we were together. It was as a family and as a city that we would join forces and resist all that was thrown at us.

Right: Aren't the British amazing? Is it something in the water or is it learned at mother's knee? Whatever the reason, it turns out to be that 'never say die spirit'. Here we are, just after the first major air raid on the city during the war. Our homes have been bombed. Our work places have been destroyed. A few minutes ago we were glum and miserable. We shared tales of horror and destruction. We marvelled at our good fortune in sheltering from the rain of death that fell. Then, along came the soup wagon and a little ray of sunshine was brought into lives that had been turned upside down overnight. A cold and wet day it may be, but a hot drink can warm our hands and our insides and help us face adversity with a smile. Perhaps those are bacon butties that are being munched. With that inside us we are ready for whatever Herr Hitler and his war machine can throw at us. During the war everyone had his or her part to play. Whilst the troops were at the front line, those left behind played their part in reserved occupations, such as the munitions factories. But, the value of the voluntary forces, driving rescue vehicles and mobile canteens, was not to be underestimated. Sometimes in difficult and dangerous circumstances, their support was vital to those who had lost their homes. The relief they brought gave others the heart to battle on. What had been born as the 'Dunkirk spirit' for those involved in rescuing the troops from France, became a reality for all when war touched us directly.

Left: Nose first in the dirt. Someone's pride and joy; brightly polished coach-work and gleaming chrome, now just another statistic of the blitz. Seventy-five per cent of local industry had been hit. Some 45,000 houses had been lost or damaged. The only surprise was that the death toll wasn't higher. Fortunately, many had taken to the shelters or were living out of town at night. The wailing sirens of the evening before had warned of the attacks. Even so, no-one was really ready for what was to fall. The cloudless sky had provided perfect conditions for the German navigators to find their way and for the bomb aimers to lock on to their targets. Much Park Street was just one of the many that greeted its residents with such a sight the next day. Craters in the streets, windows blown out and roofs ripped off. Not much of a welcome home to find that all you had worked for over the years had been blasted to smithereens. ARPs and wardens did their best, but it was a hopeless task for them. 'Put that light out' wasn't much use when the fires were raging unchecked. It was frustration in being unable either to protect what you had or to hit back that got to you. Stories in the papers and clips on the newsreels gave some idea of what it was like to be blitzed. But nothing prepared you for the stark reality.

Below: The armistice had been signed. The boys were back from the front.

Now began the mammoth job of revitalising the city. To do that a huge building programme was begun. Plans were thought up and consultation made. It was to be a long, expensive and drawn-out process. The first thing to be done was to level as many sites as possible. In the meantime, business had to be carried on as close to usual as could be managed. Shops and stores had to continue to trade to stay afloat. They couldn't suspend trade until the city centre was overhauled. So, in 1946, Smithford Street was a mixture of cleared sites, shops still operating and those that had adopted temporary premises. Towards the top of the street Hilton's footwear shop was still open. However, if you wanted a 'titfer' to go with the pair of demob shoes you had just got, then give your legs a stretch. Dunn's, the cap and hat-maker, had moved to a new home. Signboards, like the one at the bottom left, were springing up all over the place. Shopowners couldn't afford to lose custom. They needed to keep the customer informed to maintain continuity. There would be plenty of other businesses opening before too long. They wanted those jealously guarded ration coupons, too. Some of the temporary premises were no more than a just about functional stopgap. All shapes and sizes of wooden and tin huts appeared. Corrugated iron prefabs sprouted around the former commercial centre. It looked, at times, like a

How could they? What have we done to deserve this? Questions on the lips of bewildered churchgoers as they view the scene of destruction. Local residents gaze in disbelief at the havoc wrought by the Luftwaffe bombers. What had been a proud and sacred place of worship was now reduced to a pile of charred timbers, twisted metal and rubble. This was the sight that greeted visitors to

Coventry's St Michael's Cathedral in the aftermath of the air raid of November 1940. Goering's bombs ripped the heart out of the city, but fire attacked its very soul. Only the outside walls and the tower remained standing. The style of architecture was the result of 14th century rebuilding in the perpendicular Gothic style. Further remodelling took place in the 1880s. However, St

Michael's had been more than a symbol of religion. Until becoming a cathedral in 1918, when the diocese of Coventry was formed, it had been one of the largest parish churches in the country. Despite its new status, the cathedral retained its parish feel. Members of the congregation regarded it as their own. What did it matter to those in a state of shock, walking around the ruins, to learn later that this was Britain's only cathedral to have been destroyed in the war. That was no consolation. At this moment all we wanted to do was to turn back the clock. Then we could have our lovely cathedral back. War isn't like that. It has no sentiment or magic. Coventry came to the same stark conclusion that fateful night.

Above: The planes have gone and life is returning to normal. That is, if you can count having the heart of your city ripped out as normal. It is 1941. The buses pick their way through the debris. Two major air raids devastated Coventry in late 1940 and the spring of 1941. The view from the cathedral tower shows a sombre picture of wartime Britain. Many buildings that weren't flattened by the bombs were pulled down because they were unsafe. It was a constant reminder to the bus passengers on their way into the city of how close death and destruction was to them all. It had been the incendiary devices, rather than the high explosive bombs, that had created most havoc. Householders had stayed out of harm's way, alerted by the sirens. But, while in their Anderson shelters or wherever they had sought refuge, fires raged unchecked. There weren't enough firefighters or appliances available to cope. All they could do was their best. When people returned to their homes many found only burned out shells. The rubble still around them as they travelled through Coventry only acted as a sad reminder of what had been lost. It did, though, harden the resolve to rise from the ashes and resist whatever the enemy had in store for the future. Rebuilding would have to wait. There was the winning of the war to be achieved first.

The wreck that once was proud Broadgate can be seen looking west across the city. The dust and debris of the city centre was to become a customary sight as the war dragged on. The air raids of November 1940 and April 1941 left little that was recognisable from the days before hostilities began. The drone of the bombers had gone away, but their calling card had been left in a terrible way. The tower of the market hall stands alone in the midst of the carnage. It points an accusing finger at the skies that once were thick with Junkers and Heinkel planes. Revenge would come in strikes like the 1,000 bomber raid on Cologne in 1942. This only led to the tit for tat flying bombs and doodlebugs. There are no winners from war, only survivors.

Before the war, it had been recognised that changes had to be made to the Barracks Market. The raids made sure that would now have to happen. The wholesale and retail sides of the market had become too unwieldy to function efficiently together. They would have to be separated. Eventually, a fish, fruit and vegetable market was built at Barras Heath. The nearby railway line made sure that a direct link to the outside world was available. More produce could be brought in and at a quicker rate than had been possible via the road network.

Below: Over a year has gone by since the major air raids flattened the city. The wreckage remains an eyesore, but there is little point in putting it back together. Who, in 1942, could guess when the time would come to put it back together? Singapore had fallen to the Japanese. The desert war in North Africa continued and the Russians were under invasion. Hitler had said that he wanted every English town in the Baedeker guide book razed to the ground. It was hard to think ahead to a day when things could get back to normal. Families flocked to the church to gain some comfort in prayer. By some miracle, the church of Holy Trinity had escaped with only minor damage. Its famous spire, rising high above the impressive timbered ceiling, seemed to mock the planes that flew above. It pointed an accusing finger as to say, 'I'm still here. We're still together.' The people thanked God for its reprieve and, under the medieval 'Doom' wall painting, asked that their boys overseas would come back safely. For many, that wish would take another three years to be granted. For others,

the prayers would not be answered. In the meantime, they waited. A cup of tea in the corner café might help. There was something in the British that made us settle on a cuppa in times of stress. It was a comfort, a slice of normality. Pearks' stores van whips along to its next delivery, keeping the shelves stocked with more.

Bottom: The water from the fire engines' hosepipes still glistens on the north end of Broadgate. The Owen & Owen store (now Alders) had only been open for three years. Now it stands above the scene of carnage. Its heart has been ripped out by the incendiaries that burst within it. The night before, the emergency services had been stretched beyond their limits. They were just unable to cope with the volume of the explosives that rained down from the skies. Throughout the raid, volunteers backed up firefighters and ambulance drivers. Even so, the level of destruction was immense as fires raged unabated. On this dank, dark morning in the middle of November 1940, local residents can only gape at the remnants of what was once a fine city centre. The previous day it had been a place to shop and carry out your business. What a difference a day makes. All that is left are piles of bricks and concrete dust. Lorries start the long task of moving the debris and bringing down the remaining shells of buildings that totter precariously, ready to join their neighbours that have already fallen. Hope of finding any more survivors has largely gone. Over 500 have died. The number will more than double with the coming of further raids the following year. Meanwhile, the German planes are safely back in the fatherland, getting ready to refill their bomb chambers with more weapons of death. They will be meant for Manchester, Birmingham or London. Pity the poor souls who live there. We know how they will be feeling to-morrow.

Lee Beesley - the specialist electrical and mechanical engineers

In the early days when few enjoyed domestic electricity, electricians and carpenters worked hand in hand to install and enclose electric wires. One such team, composed of electrician Herbert Beesley, the representative of the modern world to come, and Charles Lee his carpenter, were 'capping and casing' electric wiring for Mr William Iliffe. In the best traditions of the era, it was 1907, he noticed their conscientious workmanship, suggested they set up in business together and even rented to them part of his premises in Vicar Lane, Coventry, home of the Midland Daily Telegraph, later the Coventry Evening Telegraph.

Mr Iliffe stipulated they care for the table in their new office as Alfred Harmsworth, the future Lord Northcliffe the newspaper magnate, had used it when working for him as a reporter. Their sponsor engaged the new partners to install the first electrical wiring in his works which even included the revolutionary concept of electrical power for the presses. The first electric motor was a gas powered Direct Current (DC) generator. In 1912 this was replaced, by arrangement with the Coventry

Electrical Engineer, with a 250 kilowatt rotary converter supplied with 2,000 volts Alternating Current (AC) which it changed to 100 volts DC. The new printing presses used variable speed motors driven by this current.

When houses in towns still relied on gas for lighting country dwellers continued to use oil lamps. As cleaning and maintaining these in country mansions was a monumental task many stately home owners were attracted to the new electricity in order to run their homes in a more up-to-date and cost effective manner. The Edwardian period was a time of innovation when cars were beginning to replace horses and tradesmen with skills in the latest technologies were setting up to make their fortunes, just as today.

The Lee Beesley team installed generators, storage batteries and wiring circuits in a number of Midland country houses including Mr Iliffe's home

Below: *Lee Beesley's original premises on Smithford Street, pictured on the right.*

Allesley House in nearby Allesley, now the Allesley Hotel. The new partners recorded in their wages book that they drew £1. 17s. 6d (£1.87p) each in their first week together. A year later they took on their first apprentice, 14 year old Harry Terry, he became a qualified tradesman in 1915 and stayed with the company until he retired in 1959. Well aware of their responsibilities as employers Lee Beesley and Co joined the Electrical Contractors Association in December 1914, eighty five years later they are one of the oldest electrical firms in membership.

Not only did the partners install wiring circuits but they undertook regular servicing work for customers as there were few companies able to employ their own electricians.

The halcyon days of the Edwardian Summer gave way to the grim years of the Great War when Lee Beesley were heavily engaged in modernising ordnance factories with electrical installations. Came the long awaited Peace and the twelve year old company reluctantly left Vicar Lane for larger premises, next to the new City Arcade, in Smithford Street. Here they had shop, workshop and stores on the ground floor capped by two floors of offices plus a van and two handcarts, the latter a common sight at the time.

The industrial development of Coventry between 1920 and 1935 was considerable, particularly in the motor industry which had a number of small car

producers in the nearby village of Balsall Common. All the modern factories being built on the new by-passes around old towns and in the fashionable Garden Cities were powered by clean efficient electricity. Steam belonged to the past while Lee Beesley was part of the modern world in tune with the spirit of Art Deco exemplified by flats and semis, cinemas and public buildings, suburban trains and milk floats all run by electric power.

For all the peace at any price compromises of the 1930s His Majesty's Government, prompted by visionaries such as Winston Churchill, embarked on a programme of shadow factory building to provide industrial capacity away from cities likely to be targeted by enemy bombers. Lee Beesley was heavily involved in these projects including wiring and equipping a brand new airscrew (propeller) factory near Gloucester and the first air frame factory on the edge of Liverpool where the Blenheim bomber was constructed. When Charles Lee, the carpenter, retired in 1937 the firm was turned into a limited company. Overall it was was involved in electrifying three quarters of the factories built for the powerful Ministry of Aircraft Production.

Top: A 1955 Daimler Conquest roadster and one of Lee Beesley's fleet of vans visiting the Jaguar plant, one of the company's major customers.
Above: An early letterhead.

The second world war, for all its restrictions and shortages, provided a bonus for companies such as Lee Beesley whose well trained electricians were classified as working in a reserved occupation. Where other businesses lost men called to the colours Lee Beesley, by virtue of doing work of National Importance, gained men who were directed to its projects around the country. The building and equipping of five hundred airfields plus the dispersal and re-equipping some eight hundred factories relied in considerable part on electrical contractors of the calibre of Lee Beesley.

Much of the work done was classified as Top Secret so that staff had to be vetted by MI5 in order to work in hush hush sites such as that where the Gloucester Meteor, Britain's first jet propelled fighter, was developed. Housing staff was

frequently a problem where factories were relocated so many country houses were conscripted and turned into hostels. During the 1940 Blitz of Coventry many of the car workers drove out of the burning city to catch a few hours sleep in country lanes before returning to shifts in damaged works. Such was the spirit and determination that full production was often achieved within days of a raid and, when necessary, subsequent relocation.

The post war years saw Coventry City Centre rebuilt in the imaginative, even controversial, style of the New Elizabethan Age. The company expanded by setting up branches in Birmingham and Swansea in 1951, Festival of Britain Year and a long association with the Ryton car manufacturing plant began with the Rootes Group, then Chrysler and in recent times Peugeot. The Liverpool branch was established in

1953, Coronation Year, and a rebuilt Plymouth became a Lee Beesley outpost in 1960, the start of the Swinging Sixties.

The Gloucester factory manufactures plant such as electronic control systems and also builds and tests prototypes prior to full production. It specialises in the design and manufacture of precision machinery and it also produces sheet metal which can be stove enamelled on site. Here were produced portable electric powered air conditioning pumps for use in Far Eastern hospitals. From this developed the requirement for cooling radar installations and the enclosed cabins where the operators worked.

Working from connections made in

Left: *Lee Beesley have provided electrical engineering services to the Ryton Plant for more than 40 years. Today it is home to Peugeot.*

equipping aircraft factories Lee Beesley started a programme of making test rigs for the aero industry. Their brief was to provide equipment to test fuel systems, aircraft gears and propeller feathering pumps plus the heavy duty vibratory jacks to test the then little known concept of metal fatigue. The latter, so graphically described by Neville Shute, literally caused wings to fall off fuselages of aircraft in mid flight. Lee Beesley also set up the first supersonic wind tunnel to test aircraft behaviour in Britain.

To cope with an unprecedented need for replacement housing redundant aircraft factories were converted to the manufacture of the soon to be famous prefabs. These small but well planned prefabricated bungalows were made of aluminium, insulated with foam, then a revolutionary concept, and fully equipped with built in storage units. They were designed with homeless families in mind and proved so popular that many are still inhabited in the 1990s by people who refuse to leave them. The pioneering production methods used in making these funny, not quite ugly and yet totally homely little cottages of the 1940s and early 50s were the fore-runners of those used ever since in building schools, offices, factories and tower blocks of flats.

Although Herbert Beesley was a pioneer in his day he would probably be astounded at the scope and variety of the enterprises run by the company which he, in co-operation with a carpenter, founded in

Above: The maze of wiring at the Longbridge Mini Metro plant. *Below:* A general view of the MV Switch Panel and Distribution Cabling at the Mini Metro Plant.

This picture: New printing presses being lifted into the Coventry Telegraph building, for which Lee Beesley supplied all the electrical services.

1907. The company's expertise in control mechanisms brought it a contract to provide and install fully automated facilities for painting and varnishing sewing machines made at the Singer factory in Glasgow. These were set up in a tunnel-like cubicle to provide cost effective control of the entire operation. Having started with sewing machines it was a small step for Lee Beesley to extend the production of the marque into specialist equipment for painting refrigerators, motor cars and other items made by mass production methods. George Nott who was Managing Director of Lee Beesley in the 1950s sought to diversify and expand the company in an extraordinary way by purchasing a Cross Channel Ferry from Captain Townsend. This was followed a few years later with the acquisition of a Norwegian Ferry company, Thoreson and the European Ferries Company was established. Lee Beesley became a subsidiary of European Ferries and undertook the design and implementation of the electrical systems of a number of Cross Channel Ferries until the company was sold in 1976.

A totally unique one-off job was the building to order of a pair of bogies, each weighing 17 tons and proofed against the corroding ravages of sea water, to provide a ship to shore link for commercial vehicles in situations where normal Ro-Ro (roll on - roll off) facilities do not prevail.

On a national scale Lee Beesley employs over 2,000 based at the Coventry head quarters and the five branches. The premises in

Right: Lee Beesley designed and supplied the test rigs for Lear Seating who produce car seats for Jaguar Cars. ***Below:*** *Free Enterprise V, just one of the ferries owned by European Ferries and Lee Beesley.* ***Bottom:*** *An oil filtration unit.*

Above: *Electrical installation at GKN - manufacturing Side Impact Bars for Ford Transit vans.*

Birmingham were originally in the Snow Hill area until it was planned out of existence to be mourned by older Brummies. The Public Works Committee, which had a policy of finding suitable new sites for firms dispossessed by ring road developments, offered Lee Beesley the corner of Holloway Head and Washington Street. The six storey Lee Beesley building looks out over St Thomas's Memorial Garden from which passers-by can enjoy a view of its 'effective punctuation of the neighbouring facades'.

The interior provides clear working and storage space on the first three floors where the robust construction contrasts with the glazed super-structure of the offices above.

As is the case with all the Lee Beesley units the Birmingham branch has the full capacity to cater for its important hinterland in the industrial West Midlands. From design to construction and installation of whatever the customer in any manufacturing field requires it's a case of Electrically yours Lee Beesley.

The giant production lines of Schweppes and Coca-Cola are fully automated thanks to the ingenuity of Lee Beesley designers and engineers. The famous garden factory at Bournville, home of Cadbury's delicious Chocolates and the scene of that stunning tourist attraction Cadbury World, has been electrified with a state of the art production and packing

line by Lee Beesley. These areas are operated with automotive and pneumatic (air driven) control technology to work the conveyor systems. The modern food processing industry which changes the shape, appearance and even the taste of food from farms and market gardens to suit the marketing trends of the Millennium relies exclusively on electric power.

Cleanliness is a must as far as production supervisors, factory inspectors and the public are concerned when it comes to food processing. Many a housewife would envy the vast stainless steel vats and pans and the generous space of the spotless floors upon which no muddy dogs, messy children or careless husbands are ever permitted. Food factories of this standard are totally air conditioned with electrically monitored temperatures that preclude the existence of any airborne bacteria. Good lighting to 100 lumens per square foot, which is well above the norm required, enhances the working atmosphere so vital to maintaining rigorous standards. Humans are at their best when working conditions are right and the PLC technology, SCADA and other Networked Systems installed by Lee Beesley enable employers to attract the best staff for the job.

In all industries, as in any field of human

endeavour, there is an element of danger which thanks to Lee Beesley engineers has been reduced to the minimum. Electricity is a wonderful servant but a risky master. Lee Beesley's safety policy is to provide and ensure safe working conditions at all times while encouraging employees to follow safe working guidelines in all the work done for the company's clients.

The firm's industrial clients value a firm whose qualified engineers listen to clients who are experts in their own fields. By doing so they can co-operate in designing and producing systems which not only adhere to rigorous electrical standards but, of equal importance, provide the customer with a working system which suits the particular needs of their production enterprise. Any business will judge its suppliers by the names and reputations of their clients. A firm which regularly counts firms such as Rolls Royce and British Nuclear Fuels Limited among its clientele needs no further introduction to those who know the worth of such high performance and safety conscious manufacturers.

As Britain moves towards enhancing whatever Pan European trading and/or parliamentary links the future holds Lee Beesley is already there.

Continuous upgrading of staff skills at all levels helps to keep Lee Beesley ahead of the constantly changing requirements of those to the fore in using advanced technology. Without electricity, let alone trained technicians, all the computerised production systems, data processing, automated production lines and associated instrumentation in use today would be utterly useless. Remember the Three Day Week in the strike harassed 1960s when thousands worked in the light of candles and oil lamps in unheated buildings.

Trains, aircraft, ships and motor vehicles, offices and factories, many shops and most homes would stop functioning without the electrical gadgetry which controls almost every aspect of our daily lives. That such unimaginable disaster does not befall us is thanks to Lee Beesley, and others, who design, produce and, above all, maintain the machines that manage our lives in a world which has successfully, and electrically, sent man to the moon and back.

Lee Beesley's Project Management contracts will lift the burden of project fulfilment from the client as teams will progress schemes to install every type of electric circuit plus the control panels necessary to operate the electrical and mechanical machines. This is backed by fully computerised testing in compliance with the Health and Safety Executive's rules to ensure the safe operation of all High Voltage transformers, the wiring systems which carry the lower voltage current and the ubiquitous portable appliances which are plugged into wall sockets wherever needed. The company's Industrial Maintenance Package will care for client's electrical plant be it existing stock installed by others or systems designed, made and installed by Lee Beesley. The tailor-made service provides the level of care and expertise demanded by each customer as some may prefer regular maintenance by their own electricians calling upon Lee Beesley only in emergencies while others take out a measured term contract. The latter offers a scheduled programme of maintenance and replacement to keep the wheels of industry rolling at all times far removed from the erstwhile clock winding contracts stately home owners once had in the days when Mr Lee and Mr Beesley set out to run their own business.

Visitors to robot operated car production lines and clinical state-of-the-art breweries expect electricity to be the source of power. The mile long buildings containing vast trough-like continuous flow steel furnaces full of red hot liquid metal may appear almost too primeval for electricity. And yet the high-tech rolling mills of the same complexes where great ingots of white hot metal are turned, by pummelling and rolling, into rail lines, girders and even electrical wire, merely by the flick of an electric switch show to what extent electricity has taken over from teams of sweating men and mighty steam engines.

Since 1907 Lee Beesley has believed that whatever can be done can be done better by electricity. The firm looks forward to the future with the same confidence it has always had as a pioneer of a cleaner, more efficient, labour saving way of life for mankind.

Below: *Peter Rooney, Managing Director.*

Around the city centre

Above: In what is now the area of the upper precinct, there was once a view from High Street along the old Smithford Street. It was around here that the Presbyterian movement had a strong hold. Baptists and Congregationalists also had their roots in other pockets of the city. Followers of the beliefs of the reformer, John Calvin, might have found something dreadful in having a large 'watering-hole' in the middle of their patch. However, it remained as a temptation to be resisted. This was just as well. In 1931, the years of the depression still lingered. Money was hard to come by. There was many a wife who saw the week's housekeeping disappear down her husband's throat. Religion often blossomed as a refuge from the hard times.

It is an age since the bobby has been seen on regular point duty on the streets of our towns. Once upon a time he was a regular sight. The flashing white gloves would direct and beckon with regimental precision. As traffic increased, the long arm of the law did a valuable job at these sorts of junctions. There weren't as many traffic lights as there are today. Accidents at busy crossroads had become more frequent. At times, it was as if trams, cars, lorries, bikes and pedestrians were battling it out to see who would come out on top. It was time for the good old copper to take a hand, or, in his case, a glove.

Below: So little time and so much to do. Princess Elizabeth will soon be here. Lorries rush off to collect another load of planks and scaffolding. The grandstand and its awning need to be in place. She will take centre stage, of course, but the mayor, VIPs and other honoured guests need to have pride of place. You can't expect England's future Queen to stand on a soapbox! Miles of cable will have to be laid so that microphones and loudspeakers can be fixed up. Streets must be swept, litter cleared and flags hung. Traffic has to be re-routed and buses laid on to bring in the hordes who will be anxious to get a glimpse of the young princess and her husband of just a few months. Everything must be just so. This is a chance to show the country that Coventry is a city that can recover from the disasters of the war. The green of Broadgate is fenced off. The grass and flowerbeds have had a posse of gardeners fall upon them. Weeding and planting, cutting and mowing, they have spruced up the centrepiece so well. We can't have that work undone by heavy feet tramping all over it. It looks a busy scene now, but the hundreds going about their business will be multiplied more than tenfold come the great day. The city has echoed to the sound of hammering and banging for ages as the rebuilding process began. This time, it's so that we can share our joy with Her Royal Highness. The eyes of the nation will be on us. Now, where's that red carpet?

Stroll along the upper precinct and you're on top of a slice of history lost to us forever. The ghosts of the shops at 71-74 Smithford Street are under your feet at this very moment. Some of the names, like Burton, may still be around, but the style of living is very different. Back in 1934, the old and the modern worlds lived happily side by side. It was still an era when real horsepower was able to meet that of the motor car. Throw in the leg power of the bicycle and you have it all in this one small snapshot. Nearly everybody wore headgear then. The men sported caps and trilbies. They wore them as a sort of uniform of their social class. Styles changed very little over the years. Not true for the fairer sex. Every fashion swing brought something new.

The flapper rage of the 20s brought the cloche hats, but these had been replaced by ones with wider brims. Women also used their hats as a sign of gentility. It was rather racy to go around bareheaded. That attitude persisted for years. Even when hats were going out of fashion, there was still the phase of the headscarf to go through.
The Black Bull Inn was along Smithford Street. It had been bought for £2,000 by the government in the 1790s, during the Napoleonic wars. It was converted into a barracks. Later, the Royal Field Artillery and the 7th Battalion of the Royal Warwickshire Regiment occupied it. In 1922 it became a market and is now the site of the Barracks car park.

This is Britain's industrial heartland. Looking north, across the city in 1931, the factory chimneys on the horizon belch out their smoke. The difficult times of the late 20s are gradually being left behind. Unemployment will soon begin to fall. The work-place will fill once more and the cars roll off the assembly lines. The Clean Air Acts of the 1950s helped produce a healthier environment. The grime created by those coke-burning monsters would be a thing of the past. Living in the shadow of those chimneys meant, in the pre-war days, that shirt collars and cuffs were always mucky. Bright summer dresses were soon spotted with black flecks. Monday's washday was a busy time for Mum and the

dolly tub and mangle. Down below, on the roads in and around Broadgate, people on the go had little time to think of these matters. The word 'ecology' meant nothing and 'environment' was something to do with wild animals. Coventry was into the second quarter of the century. The times they were a-changin'. The horse and cart might still appear on the street, but their day was nearly done. The horse-less carriages were the future. So, what if there was a bit of dirt in the air? Where there was muck there was brass. The city's prosperity was based on the grit of its factories. A few filthy frocks meant that the wheels of industry were turning. With it, we could put some cash in our pockets.

Below: Waiting patiently at the bus and tram stops or on street corners was the only occupation for many in the late 20s and earlier 30s. Unemployment was high then. By 1935, though, things were looking up. Industry was booming and there were fewer idle hands to be seen. Here, on the east side of Broadgate and Cross Cheaping, it is not only the shoe prices that are coming down. The property is destined for the same fate! Across the way, the famous Midlands' brewery of Mitchell's and Butler's was guaranteed to do good business. It would be one of the outlets for the extra shillings in the weekly pay packet that the likes of aircraft workers were getting. Britain was expanding the RAF as fears about German rearmament were starting to be felt. Some of the street names, like Cross Cheaping and the nearby Ironmonger Row, gave hints of the earlier businesses carried out there. Links with more distant times on Cross Cheaping were made the previous century. A ten inch marble statuette, probably of Roman origin, had been dug up there. It was a representation of the god, Mars. He was holding a wheatsheaf and a shield. This was said to show the connection between the land and metalworker of the day.

Leading away from here is the entrance to Trinity churchyard. Holy Trinity is Coventry's only true medieval parish church. It was established in the 12th century. Its spire rises to 72m (237 ft), one of three major ones overlooking the city. It was to be fortunate to escape with only minor damage in the wartime blitz.

Above: The wide, modern esplanade and imposing ornate lamppost linked the old and the new. Following the clearance of the slums, movement on the city streets became much easier. Gone were the cramped houses and little shops on narrow, twisting lanes that fed into the centre. The traffic could now flow freely. This is the junction of Corporation Street and Hill Street as it looked in 1939. There used to be a worsted-spinning mill on Hill Street. Further along, the Society of Friends (Quakers) had a meeting house and a burial ground could be found. Coventry's varied religious groups held sway in different parts of the city. St John's Church stands on this corner. During the 17th century Civil War, prisoners were kept here. The local population was said to have been unfriendly towards them. The saying 'sent to Coventry', meaning to be ignored, probably began in this period. The church also served Bablake. This was a charity school, built to educate poor boys. Here, there are some of the few links with history still standing. Old almshouses escaped both the developer and the bomber.

Sad to say, the work of planners and builders would count for very little. This stretch of road had only just been opened when war was declared. It saw only a few months of normal activity before the blackout would come. One year further down the line and another blueprint would have to be drawn up. The 20th century gave Coventry architects more to do

Above: Coventry's skies were filled with the jibs of cranes blotting out the horizon. By 1955 rebuilding was still in full swing. It shows how huge was the task of putting the city back together. It was now 10 years since the war had ended, but there was work yet to be finished and some not yet begun. Construction companies, like McAlpine, had become part of a boom industry. It wasn't just in recreating order out of chaos on bomb sites in the nation's cities, but there were housing estates to be built and new roads to be laid. The job market had expanded so that unemployment was low. Businesses would soon snap up the new shops and offices planned for the city centre. These would be prime sites and people had money to spend. Smithford Street was home for the White Lion pub. Its mock Tudor frontage looks totally out of place, hemmed in as it is by modern offices, scaffolding and that shop which typifies England in the 20th century, Marks and Spencer. Michael Marks had begun trading from a market stall in Leeds. He moved to Wigan and teamed up to form the first Marks and Spencer store there in 1894. It was from that base that the empire spread to outlets in every large town in the country. But the drinkers in the White Lion weren't too bothered about shopping or the work going on around them. The chat in the smoky taproom and the rattling of the dominoes were of more

interest.

Right: Dirty old town. No thank you, the planners of Coventry had decided. So, the old and scruffy shops and houses around Broadgate had to go. By 1939, Trinity Street had been cut out, its official opening having taken place a couple of years earlier. Road schemes abounded at the time. The need to expand the transport system, both public and private, was rightly seen to be of importance. Newer and better road systems would have a two-fold benefit. Firstly, it would improve the flow in and around the city, attracting more business and trade. It would be easier to ship out goods manufactured here. Secondly, it would boost the motor industry, which was a vital part of the local economy. The cars, trams and buses had found it hard to wend their way through the cramped streets of the 1920s and early 30s. Now we can see that, although Broadgate is busy, the vehicles have a smooth path through the centre. At the same time, shoppers have space to spread out and can rely on a comfortable ride home. It was achieved at some cost. Under the umbrella of slum clearance, many old timber and Victorian buildings had been demolished in the name of progress. It's a pity that some of them couldn't have been kept. It shouldn't have been beyond the wit of the town planner to blend in some of that history and style. But, it was a case of out with

Above: Standing on the roof of the link block gives a good southerly view of the market stalls at the Barracks. Even in 1956, parking had become a real problem. As well as designated car parks, any scrap of waste land would do as a resting place while the shopping was done. Be careful, though. Some of the uneven plots had bumps and humps that would play havoc with the shock absorbers. Many an exhaust was mangled as unwary motorists failed to negotiate the dangers of the old bomb site.

What you saved on the weekly visit to the market wouldn't offset the cost of a new silencer. Inflation was low, mortgage rates were modest and it was a time of high employment.

There might have been the odd anxious moment for mothers with sons in the forces. The Suez crisis had just broken. Apart from that, it was a time to enjoy, a period of plenty. The ration book had been put away. There was real choice to be had once more. The market stalls overflowed with good quality produce.

Cheap imports, although not helping our economy in the long run, held down prices in the shops. The austere and functional clothing of the 40s was being replaced by more adventurous styles from Europe. Gaily decorated fabrics from the East covered the counters as dressmaking became fun again. The American influence was still to come. It would, though. Shopping malls and giant 'stack em high, sell em cheap' stores were on their way. Better still, we had something to cheer about. Jim Laker had just skittled the Aussies with his 19 wickets in the Test match .

Below: A wrought iron lamp standard, cobbled streets and tram tracks were sights in all the main towns before the war. It's a quiet day in 1935 as we look north from Broadgate along Cross Cheaping. Just round the corner, a market had been held in medieval times. Further along from here is the stretch known as the Burges. It is on the east side of this area that buildings from the pre-war period still remain. Some of them had timber frames dating back over two centuries, but these had been covered with brick refronting.

The lengthening shadows tell us that day is soon to be done and the hustle and bustle of the normally busy scene has died away. This was a world where value and quality went hand in hand with politeness and gentility. Life might have been busy, but attitudes were more easygoing. Everything didn't have to be brash or done in a rush. Compare the scene you are witnessing in the photo with what it's like now. Cross Cheaping at the end of the 20th century is the home of Kentucky Fried Chicken and McDonald's fast food outlets. Pubs and bars along the Burges now include the Coventry Cross, which advertises real ales and Sky television as equal attractions! The Tudor Rose is also there. It is a 'themed' establishment, whatever that means. Not only are we looking at a different era, but at a completely changed world.

Above: The delightful mock Tudor frontages of the shops provide an impressive backdrop to the 20th century scene. Only opened in 1937, Trinity Street led away from Broadgate towards Swanswell and did away with the older, poorer properties that had been cleared in the name of progress. At the height of the shopping day the awnings have been drawn down above the windows. There are valuable and perishable goods on display. They need protecting from the rays of the sun or they will fade or go off. Getting the hooked pole from the back and pulling down the canopy was one of the shopkeeper's first jobs at this time of year. The taller of us often had to be careful that we didn't go home

DESIGNED FOR THE EXPECTED INCREASE IN TRAFFIC, TRINITY STREET WAS GOOD AND WIDE

with a sore head after bumping into one of the supporting struts. At the end of the day came the ceremonial washing of the pavement. Buckets of water swished across the paving stones and soapy water ran off in rivulets down the gutters and into the drains. Although there was little traffic, the road had been designed with some foresight. The carriageway was good and wide. There was plenty of room for the expected increase in the use of the private car. Here, the shoppers have time to stroll across the street, either on their way home or off to the next stop on their shopping lists. When was the last time you tried to cross a city street where cars are allowed at such a leisurely pace?

Right: It reminds you a little of that opening scene on TV's 'In town tonight'. The old, now sadly deceased, broadcaster, Brian Johnston wouldn't seem out of place, popping onto screen to introduce the show. The time is right, but not the place. It's not London, but the completed Broadgate of 1963. The buses and cars go round the green like figures on a roundabout. Lady Godiva, in the very centre, must have been going dizzy as she watched them turn and turn again. Every so often one would get off the ride and disappear along one of the exits. Off they went to find their way to the outskirts, only to be replaced by another one entering and joining in the fun. The fleet of buses was kept busy bringing in people and dropping them off to shop in the pedestrian-only arcades and precincts that Coventry had pioneered. The area had been totally reconstructed by this date. The congested streets had gone. The ornamental features of the central green had a freshness and brightness. They were the envy of many who came to visit and admire.

Broadgate was the hub round which the city turned. Important shopping areas took up three sides. Originally, all of these were planned to be seven or more storeys apiece. Thankfully, someone still kept a bit of common sense and they didn't rise quite that high. Big is not always beautiful.

Below: People's names have come to be used as words in the English language, often after an invention. The hoover and the biro are examples. Another is the belisha crossing. It was named after its pioneer, Leslie Hore-Belisha. It's probably a good job that it was the last part of his name that caught on or there might be a different tale to tell! Britons walking safely over these crossings got an awful shock when they ventured abroad. The crossing in a mainland European city doesn't offer the same protection. Pedestrians seem to be fair game on the continent. It is at home where the motorist waits patiently for us to cross. No-one seems to have told the cyclist on the left, however. The law, obviously, doesn't apply to him as he cuts those crossing in half! This is the junction of Hales Street and Trinity Street. The Museum of British Road Transport can now be found further down Hales Street.

To the right of this 1956 picture is Swanswell Gate. It is one of only two surviving medieval gates. Cook Street is the other. It lies on the far side of Lady Herbert's Garden. The most complete section of the city's impressive wall is to be found between these two gates. It was Edward, the Black Prince, who granted the city a licence to 'enclose the city with a wall of stone'. Swanswell was one of the minor gates scattered between Coventry's five main ones.

LONDON ROAD WAS BUILT TO CARRY A MIXTURE OF NEIGHBOURHOOD, LOCAL AND THROUGH TRAFFIC

Like an octopus spreading its tentacles or a spider spinning a massive web, the ring road snakes its way around the city. This aerial view was taken from above the island at London Road in 1971. The road was built to carry a mixture of neighbourhood, local and through traffic. Originally, links with the M6 motorway were established, as well as to other main roads to Midlands' towns. Later would come the connection with the M1 via the M69.

This area would have been in the bomb-aimer's sights back in 1940 and 1941 when it was blitzed. Neither the pilot nor his crew could have imagined the desolation that would follow the releasing of those deadly weapons. Open the bomb doors and shed the load. Then it was back home to Germany, provided the ack-ack could be avoided. Looking carefully at this picture acts as a reminder that little of pre-war Coventry remained standing. Within the centre, about the only building to have escaped intact was the NatWest bank. The nave and spire of the old St Michael's Cathedral were left standing as a form of memorial of the war. The new cathedral was rebuilt alongside in 1962. It is, though, the ruin of the former St Michael's which acts as the reminder of the futility of conflict. More than that, it offers a hope of reconciliation and a plea for the

Left: The sign in the centre states the obvious. It was hardly necessary to have been warned of road works ahead. The guard rails on the pavement kept pedestrians channelled away from danger. The towers of scaffolding and reinforced pillars had been there for all to see for some months. They would continue to dominate Broadgate and its surrounds for some time to come. The main street area had been opened in the late 1940s, but the erection of the buildings only got into full swing in the early 1950s. Broadgate House, seen here in the first stages of construction, wouldn't be completed until 1953. That would be a significant year for all Britain, as well as Coventry. To those of us who are now middle-aged or older, it was one of those special years that we remember fondly. There was a new monarch to crown. The young Elizabeth was to begin a reign which would see her, next to Victoria, as the second longest serving Queen we have had. Edmund Hillary and Sherpa Tensing climbed Everest. We won the Ashes back from the Aussies. The lovely Marilyn Monroe sang about diamonds being a girl's best friend. And who could forget the Matthews final, when Blackpool beat Bolton? It seems appropriate that the first building for the new city centre to be completed should be in that momentous year.

Above: The straight lines and foursquare look of the architecture is typical of the 50s. It gives the impression of some sort of giant Lego construction. Each piece slots ever so neatly into the next. Large housing estates were just the same. The American folk singer, Pete Seeger, summed it up in his song 'Little boxes'. He sang of 'little boxes made of ticky-tacky, and they all look just the same'. It was as if individuality was to be frowned on. We were all in this together and heaven help anyone who showed a bit of a rebel spirit. Perhaps that was why actor James Dean took cinema audiences by storm. The popularity of Elvis Presley's music had its roots in the same urge of youth to be different. Elvis was just starting out, but the star of 'Rebel without a cause' had already made his mark and gone, killed in a car crash. Meanwhile, for the more sedate, there was the Market Tavern. Even this was hardly an adventurous name for a new pub on Market Way! Remember the firkin? One of the good things about the time was that beer still came in barrels. Matured in the wooden casks and hand-drawn up from the cellars, each brew had a distinctive flavour. The ale of the pressurised metal container, which was to come later, seemed much the same as any brewery could produce. No wonder CAMRA has its addicts. Unfortunately, to qualify as real ale nowadays, it has to have bits floating in it! Watch out the landlord who served it up like that in 1957. We are told that a firkin is equivalent to 40.9 litres. Now, what's that in old money?

Below: By 1956 the precinct was nearing completion. 'About time, too,' some might have remarked. It had been a long time coming. British Home Stores occupy the site on the right and Marks and Spencer the one on the left. Further on can be found the canopy that covers Lady Godiva. It is not just as a monument to the past that the old cathedral stands towering above the life of the city taking place below. It remains as a warning to future generations of the disaster that man can bring to others, but, better, it acts as a beacon of hope for the times ahead.

St Michael's has the third highest spire in the country. Only those at Salisbury and Norwich are loftier. The Earl of Chester founded it in the 12th century. Plans for the new cathedral, built alongside the old one, caused much wrangling at first. Those of Sir Giles Gilbert Scott, he of telephone box fame, brought protests from many. These included the influential Helen Rotherham. Her watchmaking firm was a well-established business and gave her views an air of authority. Eventually, it was Basil Spence who won the design plan, back in 1951. It was to be four years before work started and not until 1962 that the consecration ceremony was held. Visitors from all over the world now marvel at the interior where Sutherland's 'Christ in Majesty' dominates the scene.

Left: The glass front of the Earl Street civic centre is typical of post-war architecture. Gone are the gloomy, but ornately fronted, offices of the early 1900s. The natural light of the newer block provided a more pleasant working environment. What was lacking in character was offset by convenience. Unfortunately, architects have seldom been able to marry the two together. The centre provides work for many council employees. It is the hub of the city's town and country planning department. It doesn't matter whether you are a householder or a property developer. This is where you send your application for a new conservatory or housing estate. Officers will visit the sites of potential development and then make recommendations to elected members in council. The education department has offices here. You are entitled to free meals for your child at school? Send in the form. You want special secondary schooling? Send in the form. You want a grant for further education? You've guessed it - send in the form. Opposite the Dillons bookshop, the Council House offers a contrast of style. It dates from the First World War. The ornate corner clock and the statues of Godiva, Leofric and Justice above the main entrance are a reminder that there is a history and tradition to the city. It can be found if you look beyond the modern offices and shopping arcades. Upstairs, in the Council House, is a fine, lofty council chamber. It is reached by an attractive curving staircase.

Above: The toddler in the pram wasn't even a twinkle in dad's eye when the reconstruction of shops on New Union Street was begun. The Silver Cross of the day could double as a child carrier and shopping basket. Is that why the bairn is down one end? Dad stops to ponder the scene across the road. In the middle of the 1950s it seemed to some that their whole adult life had been dominated by the sound of the bulldozer, piledriver and mechanical drill. This young father had his childhood inter-rupted by six years of conflict. His father, uncles and older brothers, perhaps, had suffered at the front. Every family in the land knew someone, whether family or friend, who had not returned. Now, a decade on, what was in store for his child? By the time of the millennium, dad will probably be a pensioner and grandfather. Can he recall his hopes and ambitions for his child on that day? The new life being born into the heart of Coventry commerce was to grow side by side with the children of the 50s. It is to them we must turn for judgement on the efforts made on their behalf. It was for their future that the foundations were laid. The nipper in our photograph had a lot to look forward to. Before he or she was out of teenage, man would be on the moon and a whole new technological age lay ahead. Coventry City would even win the FA Cup! However, dad would be a grandpa by then!

Can't stop. Got to hurry. The morning rush hour is well under way. It's hardly just another morning, mind. Just a few days ago the air raid of 14th November 1940 had taken its toll. Across Broadgate the market hall tower stands as a lonely monument to what had been a thriving area of commerce. Piles of bricks at its foot will be a common sight across the city for months and years to come. An anxious mother hurries her child along the pavement. Who knows when the bombs might fall again? But, there are still shops to get to, if only one can be found to be open. Whatever the circumstances, the family has to be fed. Some factories and offices had escaped the worst of the damage. Others had reopened in temporary premises. A few struggled on in the shells of burned out properties. Life had to go on and workers are hurrying in to do their best. Some go about their business bareheaded, whilst others take the precaution of wearing their tin hats. As well as the havoc wreaked by the bombs, there was still the danger of falling masonry. It was a wise move, whether you had headgear or not, to walk well away from such insecure buildings, just in case. Many people moved out of homes close to the immediate city centre. They commuted in on a daily basis. This led to transport problems and delays. They felt that this was a worthwhile price to pay for the greater peace of mind they felt.

The Earls of Chester had once had the their manor house of Cheylsmore at the rear of New Union Street. Names like Little Park Street and Much Park Street remind us where the estate used to be. The gatehouse has survived and is now the city's registry office. It is one of the few remaining associations with Queen Isabella, wife of Edward II and grandmother of Edward, the Black Prince, who stayed at Cheylsmore Manor.

Top: Remember the bus inspector? The man on the right, looking very official in his peaked cap, is checking that the Willenhall bus is ready to move out on time. Behind it, the service to Coundon patiently waits its turn. As children we used to fumble in our pockets as the inspector hopped on board. 'Have your tickets ready, please,' meant that those of us who had travelled beyond the appointed stage were in trouble. If he didn't get on our bus, you could usually get away with it. The conductor was too busy with two packed decks to recall who had paid what and to where. When one of our pals was caught out it was no good cracking that the inspector had been kicked out of the SS for cruelty. If he heard you, you'd be thrown off as well! He was also there to check that the crews weren't on the fiddle. Actor Stephen Lewis made the part his own as Blakey in the TV sitcom 'On the buses'. Here, in 1944, one such role model is ready to do battle with the Reg Varney of his time. The old gas and electricity showrooms existed peacefully side by side. It looks strange today as they battle for each other's business. Parked outside, these vehicles were powered by Daimler engines. Gottlieb Daimler's engine had first seen light of day in 1887. The company had its base in the area in an old cotton mill in Radford. By now, it had been developed to dominate the quality market before Rolls-Royce took over that position.

Above: By the mid 1950s the reconstruction of Coventry was nearing completion. The extra spire of the crane would soon disappear and leave those with a more holy background, such as Greyfriars, to dominate the skyline once again. The construction of the shops at New Union Street gave the advantage of modern purpose-built shopping to the consumer. Neat lines, bright and well laid out retail outlets made for a pleasant day with the shopping trolley. Reincarnation was almost finished. The process had been forced by the levelling of the city in the wartime raids. It was something that wouldn't have happened on such a large scale, but for the blitz. A remodelling of the city had taken place, on a smaller scale, back in the 30s. It was unlikely to have been abandoned such a short time later without the necessity created by the bombing. The advantage gained by the shoppers was achieved at a high price. It wasn't just in the loss of life, homes and businesses. Some of Coventry's history had been blown away. Other links with its proud past had now been covered over.

Bottom: In early 1949, the wide open space of Broadgate is very different from the crowded shopping precincts and arcades of the end of the 20th century. Rebuilding the city had begun and one of the first projects was to regenerate the city centre. This took place under the watchful eye of Holy Trinity that cast its gaze over the scene below. It seems to be saying that the city needs me to remind it that here is an opportunity to be born again. From the mayhem of war may come some good order.

Although Broadgate has been open officially for nearly a year, a lot of work still needs to be done to re-establish the businesses and prosperity of the city centre. The little workmen's huts at the bottom of the photograph show that rebuilding will be a lengthy process. The loose timbers and corrugated iron fencing tell us that this area is some way from completion. Two years earlier, the Corporation had decided to buy 452 acres of land in the city centre under a compulsory purchase order. Although there were wrangles with the Government and local interested bodies, the following year over half of it was declared an Area of Extensive War Damage. This eased the way, administratively. It also helped to release some funding and grants. The rebuilding of the city could begin.

Right: A busy day on Broadgate. The similar flat lines of the buildings are typical of 50s architecture. It's as if you could pick up one block from its site and swap it for another one without really noticing. Hundreds of shoppers and office workers fill the pavements and arcades as the life of this day in 1962 is well under way. The motor car is yet to dominate travel. There are as many buses as

private cars in the photograph. Public transport was still the way to move around for most people. Passenger numbers would not shrink for another decade. It would be 20 years before changes in our travelling patterns forced a major rethink on the links between shopping and the car. These connections were to change Coventry's skyline once more. For now, in a time when Kennedy was still US president and the Beatles had yet to make their mark, further change was not in our thoughts. We could idly wonder at the destination of the limousine on the right of the picture. Was it the mayoral car on its way to an official function? Was it a wedding car, or one for a more sombre occasion? We can but guess. One thing is certain. Traffic jams were few and far between. Wherever the driver was off to, he would arrive on time. Road rage, for those held up by congestion and lines of traffic, would belong to a later and less patient era.

IN 1949 LADY GODIVA WAS GIVEN PRIDE OF PLACE IN THE CENTRE OF THE GREEN ON BROADGATE

Above: It was in 1949 that the wraps came off Lady Godiva. The legendary figure was given pride of place in the centre of the green on Broadgate with her ceremonial unveiling. Mounted on her pedestal she looked out on the redevelopment of the city. Old Broadgate had been obliterated during the war.

The siting of the subject of Coventry's best-known folk heroine in the city's focal point suggested that things were returning to normal. Business was growing once more. Although many shops were still in temporary accommodation, the day was soon to come when more established sites would be found. The hard times of the immediate post-war years were easing. Rationing was still limiting the housewife's horizons, but a more certain future was on the way for the city. Much was still to be done, but the arrival of Godiva seemed to offer a sign that the corner was about to be turned.

The bus shelters on the right, in front of the corrugated iron of the temporary shop fronts, are full of shoppers waiting for the numerous buses which carried them to and from their homes. Life had returned to normality. Before another decade had passed, prime minister Macmillan would be telling us that 'we had never had it so good'. That was not the message that caused Lady Godiva to make her famous ride. Perhaps she was preparing for this new one when she set out on horseback a second time.

At leisure

THE HIPPODROME WAS ORIGINALLY SITED ON POOL MEADOW UNTIL IT WAS REBUILT IN 1937 ON HALES STREET

Bolton has its Octagon and Sheffield its Crucible. It is Coventry's Belgrade that has the boast these others can't match. It was the first civic theatre to have been built after the war. Plays and concerts take place there on a regular basis. But, it didn't come into being until 1958, four years after this photo was taken. It was the white facade of the Hippodrome, seen from the south in the middle of the picture, which had dominated live entertainment in the first half of the 20th century. The word 'hippo' means 'horse'. In its early days, people thrilled to the equestrian shows that were put on. It was originally sited on Pool Meadow. Here great fairs had been held in Victorian times. It flourished there from 1903 until 1937, when it was rebuilt on Hales Street. Known as the home of Coventry theatre, it tried to uplift and educate public taste. Ballet and opera shows featured as part of the fare on offer. You could have George Formby and Gracie Fields down from Lancashire, but you were also getting your share of Coppelia and La Traviata. The Hippodrome was that bit different. Even when Hollywood's influence on the British night out took hold, films weren't all that was on offer. They were seen as just part of the overall variety bill. It was the dreaded bingo that killed off the old style 'Hipp'. It still remains, but the Gala clubs and the sound of 'two fat ladies' don't have quite the same ring as the jokes of Frank Randall or the 'Triumph march and chorus' from Aida.

Bottom: A line of cars parked on a boulevard is straight out of the TV series 'The Untouchables'. That show was all about America in the days of prohibition and gangland violence. However, this is Coventry and not Chicago. Al Capone is safely tucked up in Alcatraz. It's just the running boards of the cars and the side-mounted spare wheels that could belong to a different world. In 1935, when this photo was taken, the life of the English was a far remove from that of our American cousins. It had something to do with the brashness of youth. A country, that was one of our colonies 150 years previously, was still developing. We had centuries of the ageing process behind us. Two Roman horseshoes had been found on the site of the old gas showrooms (later the Equity and Law building) and Roman coins had been unearthed further on in Broadgate. What sort of history do Americans have to match that?

The depression years were being left behind. The chuffing chimneys of the factories showed that production of textiles, electrical equipment, bricks, motor vehicles and aircraft engines was leading the city towards greater wealth. Unemployment had fallen from over three million to fewer than two in the last three years. Peace and prosperity seemed to be guaranteed. Students of politics would have been more cautious. Mussolini had invaded Abyssinia and Hitler had banned Jews from public life. But on a quiet day on Corporation Street it was easier to think of the good times. Sir Malcolm Campbell had broken the world speed record in his Bluebird. King George V was celebrating his silver jubilee. Rule Britannia!

Right: A lovely summer's day has dawned in June 1959. St James' Lane, at its junction with London Road, shows the calm and peace of the age. The cyclist bowls merrily along with little traffic to worry him. Space age helmets for

pedallers were still many years away. As he trundled along was he whistling a popular song of the day? If he was, it might have been Russ Conway's 'Roulette' or 'Side Saddle'. Both were hit tunes of the year. Even that sort of music reflected easy-going times. Who today could hope to top the charts as a piano player with part of a finger missing? Especially one whose style was more suited to the pub 'joanna' than the set of Top of the Pops!

Nowadays, as countless thousands of cars whiz in and out of the city along the link roads with the M1 and M40 motorways, it becomes harder to recall the scene of 40 years ago. The leafy suburbs may still be there, but the pace of life is such that we have no time to take them in. Harking back to those days we need photographs like this to remind a younger audience of a quieter and gentler time. When did you last see a carefree young lad leaning idly against a lamp-post or only two cars in a parking space for a dozen? Come to think of it, when have you the time to look?

On the move

At the end of the 20th century, rail travel was increasing in popularity once more. Despite the need for more rolling stock and passenger complaints about the ticket prices and punctuality, the train was coming back into fashion. New companies had been formed and promised to attract more and more custom. The difficulties and costs of driving and parking the private car in the large towns forced motorists to rethink. Standing on Stoney Lane bridge, looking along the line towards Birmingham, Coventry station is in the process of its reconstruction of 1960. There seemed to be something fated about any rebuilding work in Coventry. No sooner was it finished than a great change took place. The revamping of the city in the late 1930s had been undone by the blitz. In 1961 Dr Richard Beeching would be appointed as the new head of British Rail.

His programme of branch line cuts would change the face of the local railway system over the next four years, until his sacking at the end of 1964. By then he had become Lord Beeching and half the network had been slashed.

The original track had helped connect London to Birmingham in 1838. It followed a line specified by George Stephenson. Countless contented boys and girls had stood on the platforms, whiling away the happy hours, in the aimless, but harmless, pastime of collecting engine numbers. They'd be copied faithfully into one of many exercise books and, unless the owner developed into a full-blown 'anorak', put into the loft and left to gather dust. The best treat was to stand on the bridge and wait for one of the old locos to come and whoosh steam all over you.

Left: At night, Broadgate would rattle and hum to the sound of the trams. Like two giant tin cans, these swish their way along the rain-soaked tracks and across the cobbles. The pantographs linking them to the overhead electric cables stretch out like a plant's tendrils sucking out the juice of life itself. The headlamps remind you of a Cyclops' single eye, searching out a way through the dark and murk of the city gloom. It's almost as though they are in conversation with each other as they slip side by side along their tracks. If so, their chat would be of the troubled world in which they lived. It is 1939 and the storm clouds are gathering over Europe. Mr Chamberlain will soon be returning from Munich with his hopeful, but soon to be proved useless, bit of paper. Perhaps they spoke of happier times that year. Portsmouth had beaten Midlands rivals, Wolves, in the FA Cup Final. Maybe passengers were whistling the Judy Garland song, 'Over the rainbow'. Little did they know that there wouldn't be another Cup Final for seven years. The crock of gold under the rainbow would be oh so distant. Did these trams wonder what was in store for them? They wouldn't know that they had only a couple of years of life left in them. The first trams were steam driven. They had difficulty getting up the hills around the town. Electricity opened up new routes. This tramway had begun as Coventry Electric Tramways Company, being purchased by the Corporation in 1882. By the time of this photograph, there were 55 trams in operation. Death, when it came, was sudden. The tracks were destroyed in the air raids of 1940 and 1941. Trams were mainly abandoned and laid to rest before their phasing out in most other cities in the 50s.

Below: The woman wearing the scarf is fascinated by something off picture. It is to be hoped that she has not been attracted by something known as builders' cleavage. Maybe a shirt has been removed and rippling muscles are on show. Heaven forbid! A wolf whistle might also have come her way. 'Wotcher gorgeous' was the penalty for most women passing a building site before political correctness came into the language. There would be plenty of such chances and such building sites around Coventry after the war. The rebuilding of the city was a mammoth task. Construction workers and their bosses were never short of demands on their time. If the subject of our photo were married to someone in the industry, she could be guaranteed a good tip-up when the pay packet hit the kitchen table at the end of the week. Times were getting much better. Rationing had largely gone. Jobs were plentiful. Everything seemed rosy. Ownership of the motor car was more common and a new hope was in the air. Here we are looking at the top of Hertford Street. The bridge under construction is now incorporated into part of the new pedestrianised shopping area. Look carefully today and you can see the mosaic created by Hugh Hosking, former principal at the College of Art. It shows the Coventry Martyrs who were burned at the stake in the 16th century, during the reign of Mary I.

Like a beached whale the Midland Red lies stranded. Photographed in 1940 at Digbeth Garage, this bus will run no more. The stoics of the city take it all in their stride. They look quietly with a sense of resignation at the twisted metal and broken glass that was once a shining example of the modern age. German bombs had brought this proud people carrier to its knees. The little lad looks into the top deck where he sat just a day or two ago. What jolly times he had on the top deck. Laughing with his pals, they'd share stories of silly schoolmistresses and playground games of British Bulldog. The adults would need that bulldog spirit as they tried to put their own lives back together after that fateful November night. The boy didn't have such deep thoughts. He was recalling the place he'd stuck that bit of sticky treacle toffee left over from Bonfire Night. If one of those awful girls hadn't sat on it, as he had hoped, then he might be able to rescue it for a chew later. Note the short trousers. Little boys had knees then. Cut, grazed and dirty, they were proper knees, not white ones covered up with jeans or designer shell suits. The Pool Meadow bus station of today stands on what was St Osburg's pool. She was an abbess who established a nunnery in Coventry in medieval times.

It looks as though someone has placed a large strip of a child's train track on top of a toy town. Seen from the air, this section of the inner ring road was opened in 1970. It was a much needed blot on the landscape. Traffic in the city was becoming a nightmare. The turning of the centre into a largely car free zone had meant that congestion hadn't been cured. It had just been moved to the fringes. By the time Ringway was opened, Coventry boasted 146 cars per 1,000 of population. This was almost half again the national average of 107. But with the new road, traffic could get to its destination more easily without having to clog the outlying streets. Those on the move to places further afield could avoid the jams altogether. Link junctions got you onto the roads out to Warwick, Birmingham, Leicester etc with simplicity.

This part of the road is the section above the coach park at Swanswell. To the right is the Pool Meadow bus station. As you drive along this stretch of a modern highway you will have just passed above the Museum of British Road Transport. In there is the world's largest collection of British cars, motorcycles and bicycles. It's well worth nipping off the ring road to wallow in the nostalgia of yesteryear.

Above: It didn't take big business long to find new premises when it had to. The Marks and Spencer store had been lost in the November 1940 air raid. Within the month, a temporary resting place had been found. The garage on Whitefriars Street may not have been the ideal choice, but it did nicely enough for now. The 'Marks & Sparks' empire had begun in humble surroundings on market stalls. It was not so proud that it couldn't make do with its current home. Anyway, business was business, even if there was a war on. People still needed good quality clothing and this store intended to fulfil the role of provider. Once you had lost a customer, she might not come back. The longer you stayed shut, the more likely it was that the fickle shopper would make somewhere else her regular port of call. The posh called it being pragmatic. Normal folk said it was using your common sense. The Lanchester name was used on cars right up to 1956. It had long ceased to run as a separate company. Daimler had taken it over in 1931. It continued to use the original name because of the fine reputation the Lanchester had built up. Born in 1868, FW Lanchester made his first car in 1901. It was famous for its silent running qualities. He rose to become chief engineer at Daimler. He did this while still producing his own line of cars. His interests weren't limited to the motor car. Lanchester also worked on projects connected with aerial flight and acoustics. He led a busy, interesting life that came to an end in 1946. He had played his part in the industrial development of the district.

Below: There's a draught like a mother-in-law's breath howling through here. Whoever thought of calling them bus shelters never stood in one. The wind could find its way through every nook and cranny. For some reason there was always a gap at ankle level. It was at the perfect height to blow over the top of your high heels and under the hem of your coat. The trees that lined Warwick Rd leaned over backwards in sympathy from the wind. At least the history of the area gave you something to take your mind off the discomfort of waiting for the bus to arrive. Close by is the Quadrant, an impressive curve of terraced houses in a Regency style. Further along Warwick Road stands the United Reform Church and the former Reform Club. The church was built with its Renaissance style facade around 1890. The Club, now no 5, dates from around 1820. This was quite a fashionable area in the late 18th century. The novelist, George Eliot, then Mary Ann Evans, went to school here in the 1830s.

There was plenty to think about in Coventry's past as you waited for the no 17 bus to Bagington. Your destination had its own important place in the city's life. The Armstrong-Whitworth Aircraft factory and airfield were to be found there. At the time of this picture, the AWA had just suffered a disappointment with its Apollo 31 seater plane. In trials, the larger Vickers Viscount had outperformed it. It was this aircraft which was to receive Government backing.

Shopping spree

Below: Even in 1947 there was still much to do. Damaged buildings, with their broken windows and gutted interiors, still stood as a reminder of the war. This shop had literally 'gone for a Burton' and the famous clothes' store had moved on. So, it wouldn't be to this corner of Broadgate that you would have gone for your demob suit. The Montague Burton business did good trade in fitting out the sailor home from the sea. A new set of clothes came as a welcome relief from the uniform that had been worn for so long. The phrase 'the full Monty' had come into the language. Women adopted the New Look, which was all the rage. The male of the species was still much more conservative. Dark lounge suits and heavy overcoats, topped off with a dapper trilby, were the order of the day. In some ways, the men kept to a uniform, after all. They certainly dressed in a style that was very similar to that of the next man. It was with the 50s and the greater spending power of the teenager that men's fashion would start to get a mention. Teddy boy suits and Italian style clothing hit the High Street. By the time of flower power in the following decade, with its colours and patterns, the baby boomers would have tossed aside the sombre clothes of their dads. Back in the 40s, it was only stage comics, like Max Miller or Arthur English, who could get away with loud jackets and ties. If you dressed like that in the street you'd be labelled a spiv.

Right: If you play in pub quiz teams, you will have come across the question 'Which was the last year in which we had three kings?' The answer, of course, is 1936. George V died in January and was succeeded by his son, who became Edward VIII. By the end of the year he had gone. Brought down by the scandal and controversy of his relationship with the American, Wallis Simpson, he abdicated. His brother replaced him. The year began with George V and ended with George VI. There was much heartache and heart searching in between.

This scene on Broadgate is on the occasion of the proclamation of Edward's accession to the throne. The interest in the royal family would cause large crowds to gather at the announcement of a birth, death or other major event. Cynics would have you believe that today the royals are outmoded. Nothing could be further from the truth. Just look at the millions who flocked to pay their respects to the Princess of Wales when she died in 1997. As the millennium arrives the activities of the Queen and her family provoke just as much interest as before, if not the same level of approval.

Just to make sure that the announcement being made on that day in 1936 is blessed with an air of reverence, God's house keeps a watchful eye on the proceedings from above the line of shops.

This style of arcade shopping was a common feature on Britain's high streets in the 1950s. Lots of glass and high arched ceilings gave a light and airy atmosphere in which to shop. Seen from the upper storey of the city arcade, the sale at Green's is attracting a fair amount of attention. This shop specialised in woollens, casement curtains and brocades. In earlier times Eli Green had been to the forefront of the ribbon making industry.

Going to the sales had a special feel for the housewife in the middle of the 20th century. There were genuine bargains to be had. Reduced items were sold at particular times of the year. The contents of her purse would go that little bit further. The kids could be kitted out for the year and there still might be a few bob left for some material for her. Then, it would be off back home with it to run up a new set of curtains or a nice patterned frock. The all year long sale, which always seems to be ending next Sunday, but never does, is an invention of the latter part of the century. Women dominated shopping. The menfolk went on sufferance. 'Tell you what. I'll keep out from under your feet and just nip into the White Lion for a pint. Meet you back at the bus stop.' Good old dad, always thoughtful! Mum wasn't worried. He was better there than grumbling along at her side.

Above: The city's shops and stores refused to lie down and die. Although little remained of the old premises, there was plenty of fighting spirit left. New sites and replacement buildings would be a long time coming. Until then, temporary structures, with their corrugated iron fronts, appeared all over the place. Here, in 1947, on the east side of Broadgate, the clothing trade was well represented. Servicemen back from the war could get their civvies as they changed out of their uniforms for the last time. Others could exchange their prized clothing coupons for the shirts, frocks and blouses that were available. This was always supposing the household purse contained enough. Money was tight. Times were austere. Often it was more a case of mend and make do. Hand-me-down clothes were often a family's mainstay. First up, best dressed was the watchword in some homes. Even so, there is plenty of activity around the shops. Some folk had money to spend. It was just that they didn't have it to burn. On the left, Willson's sold what were genteelly described as 'women's garments'. It seemed a little cheeky to give the name of some of these. Much fun could be had at the expense of the salesman who 'travelled in women's underwear'! Comedians of the day used this sort of gag as a staple diet in their variety acts. The large building on the left was the home to the council offices, which occupied the upper storeys. Downstairs was Martin's bank. It would disappear from the country's high streets, in time. Barclays took it over about 15 years later.

Top: Rationing is in full swing throughout the country. The hard times for Britain after the war were all the worse for towns and cities like Coventry. They had to live through the period of shortages whilst trying to rebuild and regenerate. The new Labour government had been in power for less than three years in 1948. The coming of the welfare state gave some support to the needy. The Ministry of Food advice centre gave useful tips on menus and diets. The housewife was given ideas on how to make a decent and nourishing meal from very little. Her role as keeper of the family purse became more important in making the budget stretch further in those tight days. Her skill in producing something appetising from the meagre rations allowed was to be marvelled at. There was something tasty on offer at Wilson's to keep the kids happy. That's as long as you didn't ask too closely about what was in the home-made ingredients! There might have been a surprise or two in store. Even though fresh produce was limited, the Barracks on this summer day seemed to be doing good business. The market was also a good place to meet old friends and share a tale or two in an old-fashioned chinwag. Stallholders and their cheery cries were not just a call to buy. They were part of the tradition of British life that was regaining its carefree spirit. The dark days had gone and a new dawn was on the horizon.

The Barracks market was in its death throes. It was soon to close and be demolished. It hardly looked to be on its last legs, this day in November 1958. The narrow aisles made shopping a sweaty affair as you eased your past the stacks of orange boxes and other people getting the week's fruit and veg. It was the mum's job to sort out the housekeeping and fill the basket. No red-blooded male risked being seen here. If it became known that he went to do the family shop, he'd be subjected to some rotten ribbing from his mates. What a sissy! If you were a pensioner, it was all right to join the queue, but only once you had reached that certain age. A tanner a pound, five for a shilling. Proper measures back then. How can you tell what the value is of 45 pence for 100 grams? Into the millennium and you need a degree in applied mathematics to work out the bill. Who ever heard of 250 millilitres? I'll have a half pint, thank you very much. There's something very satisfying about choosing what you buy. Point to those apples or these onions and you were in control. Now you have to have them on a crummy tray, wrapped in cellophane. Plastic wrapping, plastic food. But, nostalgia can play tricks. Didn't the apples have bruised bits that you only discovered when you got home? Remember biting into one and finding a little grub? Even worse was biting into one and finding half a grub!

At work

By 1947, Coventry's Daimler factory was in full swing and men just back from the war were eager to work there

It was the American, Henry Ford, who was mainly responsible for the development of the assembly line in motor car production. He didn't invent or originate the idea, but it was his extensive use of this pattern of working, during World War I, that saw output increase dramatically. This method was adopted and further developed by his competitors. By 1947, the local Daimler factory was in full swing. The firm's founder was a German engineer and inventor. In 1870 he helped develop the Otto petrol engine. Having become a director of the firm, in the 1880s he went on to pioneer work on the internal combustion engine.

Boredom and difficulty in meeting output targets often presented problems. The monotony of the work led to a high turnover of staff. Later, strikes and go-slows would bedevil the industry. Strong unions battled in their members' interests to secure better rates. It was sometimes said that you couldn't be sure what would be out first this Spring. It could be the daffodils or the car workers! In this photo the men are fresh back from the war. They wanted to get back to work and put some cash on the table for their wives come pay day. It must have struck some of them as funny that it was a German machine that was giving them their living. They'd just spent six years fighting them.

COMMER
COMMERCIAL VEHICLE
ASSEMBLY PLANT

ROOTES GROUP
MANUFACTURING DIVISION
STOKE & ALDERMOOR PLANTS
COVENTRY

Above: Without the obvious knowledge that this is the manufacturing plant of the Rootes Group, once known as the Humber works, the mid 1950s drawing could be of a different subject. In the centre there seems to be a watchtower. With a little bit of imagination, this might hold the guards keeping the inmates firmly inside the prison camp. It is only stretching it a touch to suggest that the workforce felt a bit like captives on forced labour. Piece work and daily rates demanded close attention to the task. The repetitive nature of the daily grind was something that would be good to leave behind. The sound of the hooter signalling the end of the shift led to something resembling The Great Escape. On the other hand, this might be the site of one of Butlin's camps that had become very popular for family holidays. The lines of chalets were laid out at Skegness and Clacton just like these. Maybe not. Imagination can only take one so far!

The precision of the layout of the plant meant that it was geared for efficiency. Mass production relied on the automatic reactions of both man and machinery. Attitudes fostered in the war were carried over into peacetime. Good order and discipline in the workers and in working practices led to a reliable product output. Competition was fierce, not just nationally, but locally, too. Other firms battled to promote their wares above the rest. As far back as 1933, the author, JB Priestley, said on a visit to the city that it was 'a thick ring of motor car and cycle factories'.

Right: Neat rows, neat lines. The aerial shot of the Rootes Group Manufacturing Division in Stoke, the former Humber works, suggests that everything is just so. Well-organised buildings and uniform housing for the workers gave off a feeling of structure and automation. Back in the 1950s the workforce would hear the morning siren attracting them to their place on the assembly line. Like little robots they'd troop in through the main gates and take their place in the process of car manufacture. There were such great names rolling off the lines in those days. The Humber Hawk and Super Snipe gave the feeling of speed, power and superiority, just by the sound of the name.

The Midlands was the centre of the country's motor industry. The Rootes brothers, Reginald and William, had started the company. Born in 1896, Reginald had trained to be an accountant. His younger brother, by 2 years, served as an apprentice in the local Singer factory. It was his mechanical knowledge and drive that led to the company acquiring Hillman. By the end of the 1920s, Humber and Commer would also have come under the family umbrella. William, later to become Lord Rootes, went back to his own 'roots' when Singer was bought out in 1956. By the time of his death in 1964, Chrysler had taken over a large part of the business. It gained full control 3 years later.

Above: *Coventry was the first large scale pedestrianised shopping centre in Britain. Under construction here is the Precinct. Work in this project began in 1951 and took some four years to complete. The Upper Precinct has two-level shopping. Despite the thoughtful planning of the time, developers still made mistakes. Access to the first floor is difficult because of the steep steps. It seems that mums and pushchairs were outside the architects' experience. Quite who they thought did the bulk of the shopping in the 50s is not recorded! Businesses have tended to occupy premises above each other, rather than side by side, in order to counter this problem. This 'vertical shopping' has sometimes confused visitors.*

This picture dates from the early days of the development. As the men on the left gaze through the scaffolding poles, they try to imagine what the end product will turn out to be. They have, perhaps, returned from service overseas. There they will have seen the ruin of old cities laid waste by the enemy war machine. They will, themselves, have contributed to the destruction of many fine buildings. Whilst abroad, it will have been a stage to be passed through. Back home, it is something to live with on a daily basis. How can those piles of bricks and planks of wood be transformed into something to be recognised and of use? Have faith. They will. It will take several years, but you are standing near where you will be measured for a new suit or a pair of winkle-pickers one day.

Right: *'And for her some scarlet ribbons, scarlet ribbons for her hair.' The textile industry was badly hit by cheap foreign imports, particularly from Asia, during the 1950s. Unable to compete, the decline was inevitable. Many businesses went to the wall. For these women, either unemployment or a change of job was the future that faced them. At this time, in 1948, their days as ribbon makers at Oakley & Cox on Queen Street were numbered. It was nothing new for workers in this field. Nearly a century before the industry had seen a slump. In 1860 the removal of import tariffs on silk goods had led to street riots. Eventually, some 4,000 weavers moved jobs. Many of them went into the new business of watch making.*

Before the days of mass production, ribbon making was a cottage industry. Husband and wife would work together in a room at the top of the house. There were two walls of almost solid glass so that the maximum amount of light could get through. This was important in making sure that subtle colour differences could be seen and any complicated patterns maintained. The same principle was carried into the factory. The large windows fulfilled the same purpose as those in the Victorian house. Pink bows for pigtails, yellow ones for bunches. 'In gay profusion lying there; scarlet ribbons, lovely ribbons for her hair.'

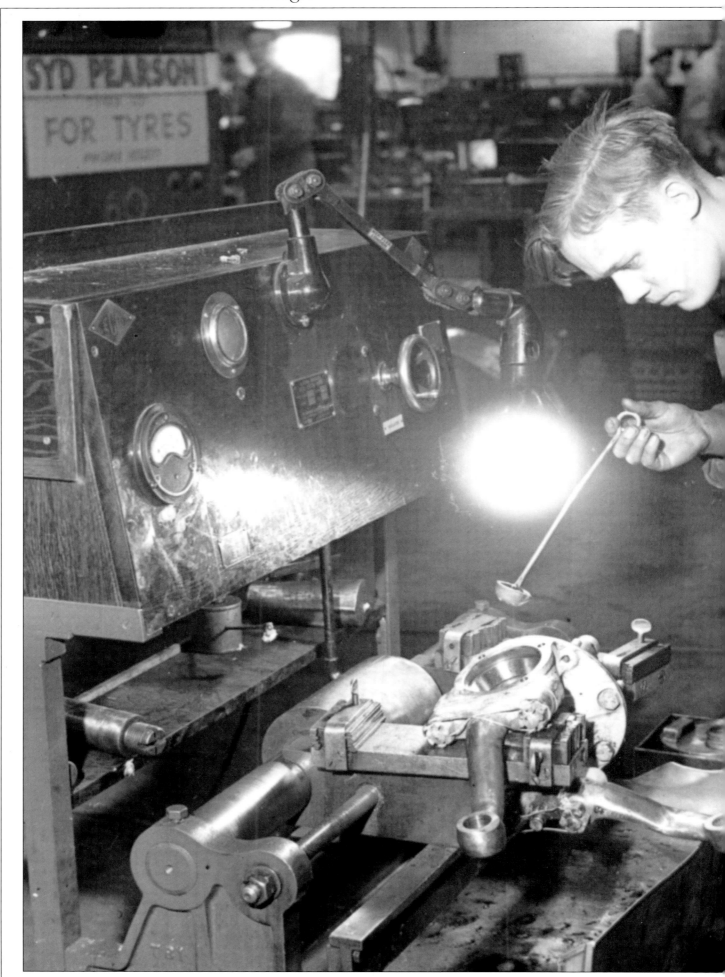

Left: Tappets and timing, bores and balancing. The mysteries of the internal workings of the combustion engine focus this young mechanic's mind in 1951. Training for an apprenticeship in motor engineering may have been begun during National Service in the armed forces and completed in the Coventry Transport Service workshop. A greasy, but necessary, job for this worker who is playing his part in keeping the city's public transport running smoothly. Before the war there had been 95 petrol driven buses serving some 37 million passengers in and around Coventry. By now, our mechanic was helping to run 304 such vehicles with no fewer than 110 million of us hopping on and off them during the year. As wage packets increased and the boom years of the late 50s and 60s came and went, the private car became more popular.

Even so, there were still 74 million fare payers during 1970.

It seems strange to see a man wearing a collar and tie whilst carrying such an oily task. It wasn't power dressing. It was a sign that he had a trade - a man to be respected. Not for him the role of a mere labourer. He had skills that he had learned in the workshop and a pride in his job. Pity his poor wife or mum who would have to deal with his messy overalls and grimy collar when he got home. Now there would have been a Daz challenge worth seeing.

Below: It took Hitler and Goering's Luftwaffe a matter of hours to blitz Coventry centre into a pile of smoking rubble. It was to take a decade of rebuilding work to repair the damage inflicted by enemy aircraft. During the late 40s and 50s it seemed as if scaffolding, ladders, workmen's huts and piles of building materials were part of the city architecture. Huge cranes, like some robots from outer space, swung across the skyline once dominated by the three spires of St Michael's, Christ Church and Holy Trinity. Dolcis Shoes seems to demand as much attention as anything sacred in this photo does. The two men on the left are so used to this scene that they stroll past without so much as an upward glance. Those on the right use the building site as a backdrop for their natter. Maybe it's more important than that. They could be discussing the work in hand. The headgear suggests a pecking order. Wear a trilby and you give the orders. A flat cap meant you did as you were told. At least you did to the gaffer's face! Touching of the forelock might have gone out of practice, but the white collar expected respect from the overall. Construction of the Precinct took most of the first half of the 1950s. It was aligned on the spire of the old cathedral of St Michael. He hadn't been forgotten.

Grace, space and pace

The word Jaguar today is likely to make most people think, first of all, of a powerful, comfortable, stylish car; or if the animal itself springs to mind, it has a way of being sleek and snarling and chrome-plated, leaping forward from back legs anchored to the bonnet of a beautiful, purring car. The marque has been in existence for more than sixty years and has built up an enthusiastic following of loyal fans both at home and abroad; regular meetings are organised by Jaguar Owners Clubs, and some of Jaguar's legendary vehicles can be seen in the Jaguar Daimler Heritage Trust at Browns Lane, a fascinating motor museum and a fine tribute to Jaguar's founder, Sir William Lyons.

The name Jaguar was first attached to sports cars in 1935, when William Lyons introduced a new range of models built on a new chassis with a new overhead valve version of the 2.5 litre Standard engine. This range was named the SS Jaguar

and superseded Lyons' earlier SS series, which had itself created a sensation at its launch at the 1931 Motor Show; there the SSI Coupe, with its ultra-low body and outrageously long bonnet, was considered phenomenal value for money - the £1,000 look for £310, as one newspaper reported. The tourer version of the SSI had also brought Lyons his first taste of international competition success, winning the the team prize in the 1933 Alpine Trial in Europe. So even the very first SS Jaguar had

Top: William Lyons, the man responsible for Jaguar Cars. Above: An advertisement for one of Lyons' Swallow Sidecars. Right: The SS Jaguar 2 ½ litre is launched in September 1935.

an illustrious reputation to maintain - which it did, in fine style.

Prior to the development of his own SS range, William Lyons had been creating stylish car bodies to fit other manufacturers' chassis for a number of years, beginning with the Austin Seven Swallow in 1927. Before that, he had designed and produced motor-cycle sidecars, a venture begun in Blackpool in September 1922, when William Lyons had just reached the age of twenty-one. William was a keen motor-cycle enthusiast, and had been greatly impressed by a stylish sidecar built by a man named William Walmseley and attached to reconditioned motorcycles. Recognising that making attractive sidecar combinations could be the basis of a sound business, William Lyons took a bank overdraft to form the Swallow Sidecar Company. His sidecars, with their pioneering use of aluminium, immediately proved popular; from sidecars he progressed to bodies for the early production cars, then to the more sporting SS range built on a chassis of his own design, and then the SS Jaguars with both his own chassis and increased-performance engines. The SS Jaguar 100 won the Manufacturer's Team Prize in the first RAC Rally in 1937; and the fact that the factory's team did not win the event outright was no reflection on the quality of their vehicles, as the winner was a privately-entered SS 100! By this time the company had moved to Coventry, and Lyons' engineering design team included William Heynes and Harry Weslake, a distinguished engineering consultant specialising in cylinder head design. Heynes, who had produced the SS Jaguar chassis, went on to improve and strengthen his design, while Weslake proceeded to develop a 1.5 and a 3.5 engine. With the 3.5 litre unit the SS Jaguar 100 could reach 60

exception of the SS 100 which was not produced again. Not surprisingly, however, it was deemed politic to drop the SS name which had acquired unfortunate connotations.

Because of various constraints in the aftermath of the war, the company launched just one new model, the Mark V, featuring Heynes' new independent front suspension system. Meanwhile, work had been going on to develop an exciting new engine, the XK, a 3442cc straight six overhead cam engine with an output of 160 hp. Feeling that the Mark V was not the appropriate car in which to launch such a high-performance engine, William Lyons set himself the task of designing a sports car for the 1948 Motor Show which was just a few months away, and the car he designed was the XK 120, considered by many to be the greatest sports car of all time. The

mph from standstill in 10.5 seconds, and had a top speed of over 100 mph, and this genuine sports car performance put it in a class of its own at that time.

The outbreak of war put a temporary stop to Lyons' developments. However, he had never stopped manufacturing sidecars, and the war brought high demand for sidecars for military use. The company also became involved in aircraft fabrication, and this introduction to the principles of aircraft design was to prove useful in the future. The sidecar division was sold soon after the end of the war, and, with the emphasis on exports, the company resumed manufacture of the pre-war range with the

Top left: *Whitley Bombers, essential wartime production.* **Below:** *The devastation caused by an enormous fire at the factory in February 1957.*

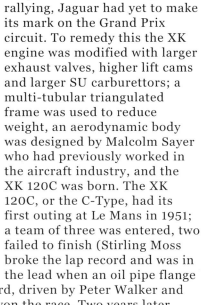

Despite success in racing and rallying, Jaguar had yet to make its mark on the Grand Prix circuit. To remedy this the XK engine was modified with larger exhaust valves, higher lift cams and larger SU carburettors; a multi-tubular triangulated frame was used to reduce weight, an aerodynamic body was designed by Malcolm Sayer who had previously worked in the aircraft industry, and the XK 120C was born. The XK 120C, or the C-Type, had its first outing at Le Mans in 1951; a team of three was entered, two failed to finish (Stirling Moss broke the lap record and was in the lead when an oil pipe flange failed), and the third, driven by Peter Walker and Peter Whitehead, won the race. Two years later Jaguar returned to Le Mans and finished first, second and fourth with C-Types fitted with disc brakes, which, being fade-free, allowed faster deceleration. This important innovation had been developed by Jaguar working in conjunction with Dunlop. Up to then, disc brakes had only been used on aircraft.

In 1954 the D-Type superseded the C-Type, and with its monocoque construction, tubular front sub-frame and aircraft-style bag tanks for fuel, the D-Type maintained Jaguar's now well-established tradition of producing ground-breaking, successful and immensely popular cars. All Jaguar needed now was a smaller, high volume model to complete its range, and this niche was duly filled by the Jaguar 2.4. Introduced in 1955, with its well-insulated unitary bodyshell and a reduced version of the 3.4

fastest production car in the world, it flabbergasted sceptics who did not believe its advertised top speed of 120 mph by clocking 126 mph at a trial in Belgium; with the windscreen removed it reached 133 mph. In a Production Sports Car race at Silverstone, one of the three XK 120s entered finished first, and another finished second; fortunately for the other competitors, the third had a puncture. Not surprisingly, orders for the car flooded in. It was just after this that the legendary partnership between Jaguar and Stirling Moss was formed, with Moss winning the Dundrod Tourist Trophy in Ulster in his first race in an XK. The XK was also enjoying great rally success, winning the Alpine Rallies in 1951 and 52 and being generally recognised as one of the most successful rally cars ever.

Jaguar's next new model, the big Mark VII saloon, was designed primarily to suit American taste - so successfully that the company had difficulty in meeting the high level of export orders from its existing factory, and as a result moved to the present manufacturing plant at Browns Lane.

Top: *The elegant 1950 Mk VII Saloon.* **Centre:** *A poster from the advertising campaign for the Mk VII.* **Right:** *The 1962 SI 3.8 E-type 260 TL.*

litre six cylinder engine, the Jaguar 2.4 provided excellent ride and refinement levels, and remained in production, in one form or another, for more than ten years.

When William Lyons retired in 1972, three years after Jaguar's merger with BMC, the company was concentrating on its sensational E-type sports range and the XJ6 range. During the early 60s many excellent saloons had been developed, but the choice of Jaguar saloon models had, it was felt, become excessive; however, the problem was solved when Lyons designed the XJ6, which was such a superb car that it replaced all other saloon models. The XJ range went on to include the XJ12 which with its V12 engine was the fastest production four-seater in the world, and Daimler versions of the XJ saloons, instantly identifiable by their fluted grilles, were also produced.

The E-type, first produced in 1961, enjoyed many years of popularity, but was replaced in 1975 by the XJ-S, a close relative of the XJ saloons, with a fuel-injected V12 engine giving a 0-60 time of 6.9 seconds.

A brief period of trouble and production difficulties in the motor industry at the end of the 70s was successfully overcome, and when the decision was made by the Government to privatise the company

and Jaguar shares were floated in August 1984, the share offer was oversubscribed eight times. Jaguar, with racing driver Tom Wilkinson, was enjoying an era of great competition success around this time; in 1882 Group 44 had designed a sports racing car around Jaguar's V12 engine, and this series, beginning with the XJR-5 and culminating in the XJR15, continued notching up memorable victories into the 90s.

Meanwhile, Jaguar has continued to enhance its superb range of cars, introducing every conceivable refinement and luxury to ensure that their appeal and competitiveness remain as strong as ever. The 1990s have seen the XJS superseded by Jaguar's new sports car, the XK8, with a completely new body design, and the new AJ-V8 engine manufactured in the all-new £125 million, dedicated Jaguar facility within the Ford Engine Plant in Bridgend. The XK8 was judged 'Best in Show' in Geneva where it was unveiled in 1996, and this model, together with the new V8-XJ range, offer today's motorist the very highest standards at value-for-money price.

Jaguar will enter the Millennium with three models, the V8-XJ range, the XK and the new S-Type sports saloon, each representing the ultimate of grace, space and pace in its own class. So, whether we own a Jaguar or just dream about it, we can look forward to seeing plenty of them on our roads in the next century.

Above: A 1977 XJ5.3 Coupe.
Left: Taking Jaguar into the next millennium, the XKR.
Below: Nick Scheele who became Chairman and Chief Executive in 1992.

Capital styles at Capitol's tiles

Over the last 30 years, Capitol Tile Supplies Limited has moved premises several times, changed its name, changed direction and grown beyond all expectations - but still has amongst its directors two of the three men who founded the company in 1968.

The early days

Prior to starting the Company, Harold Williams, his son Charles and a colleague named Ken West had spent many years in the tile industry. Between them they had a good deal of experience of the tile business and had built up a store of useful contacts, and they decided to set up their own business. They opened a small office in Hollis Road, Coventry, and began trading as the Layrite Floor and Wall Tile Company Limited. Using their detailed knowledge of all the kinds of tiles available at the time, they specialised in fixing every different type, and the firm soon established a reputation for reliability.

A year or so later Richard Davis joined the three founders, and the company added resilient flooring to its specialities. Contracts awarded to the firm increased in both number and size, bringing about a corresponding growth in the workforce; prestigious work was carried out on housing developments, swimming pools, offices and hotels. The company was by now buying in bulk, direct from the manufacturers, and this made it possible to begin a sideline in retailing and distribution. In 1972 - less than five years after the founding of the firm - the first Supatile retail outlet was opened, in Edmund Road, Coventry, and other tile centres soon followed, supplying tiles to both trade customers and to a general public which was becoming increasingly keen on DIY. It became evident that there was a great deal of scope in just supplying tiles, and in 1977 Garry Watts was invited to join the company to develop the distribution network. This enabled the two business activities, tile fixing and tile distribution, to be run as two completely separate services to the public. Between 1977 and 1985, contracting services were reduced, while on the other hand distribution continued to expand. In 1985 the firm ceased contracting and concentrated entirely on the distribution trade, becoming the Midland's leading importer and distributor of ceramic tiles and resilient flooring.

Company changes

By this time the company had moved its offices to the site of its Supatile centre in Edmund Road, and also changed its name to Capitol Tile Supplies Limited.

The next development arose out of the increase in the 'designer' market.

Above: *The Endemere Road warehouse before refurbishment.*
Facing page, top: *Harold Williams, who died in 1997, founded the company with his son, Charles and Ken West.*
Left: *The company's Endemere Road site.*

As the more progressive British and Continental manufacturers created an ever-widening range of designs, Capitol identified a need for a specific outlet to cater for the needs of interior designers and architects, and this led to the establishment of Designer Studio in Endemere Road. From here, expert staff can offer technical advice to assist with the setting of specifications, and companies who have benefited from Designer Studio's expertise include Citroen, Rover, Granada, Little Chef and Hilton Hotels.

Celebrations

Capitol Tile Group celebrated its Silver Jubilee in 1993 by holding a major trade exhibition, Expo 93, at its recently developed headquarters in Eagle Street. This was opened by the Lord Mayor of

Coventry, who also unveiled the company's new sign and commemorative plaque. At this time the Group was employing over 120 people at its three Coventry sites, and had an annual turnover in excess of £10

Right: The company's Endemere Road warehouse after refurbishment. Below: The main administrative offices at Eagle Street in the 1980s.

food processing plants. The company deals with the UK's leading tile manufacturers including Pilkington's Tiles, Dennis Ruabon, Waxman International, H and R Johnson, Woolliscroft and Daniel Platt, and overseas tile manufacturers such as the Turkish company Vitra, Iris Ceramica and Co-operativa Ceramica D'Imola from Italy, and Roca and Rocersa from Spain. Adhesives and accessories from manufacturers such as Ardex, Norcros (BAL), Schluter Systems and Homelux, and resilient flooring products from Marley and Burmatex are also stocked.

Its efforts to supply customers with the very latest products have earned Capitol Tile Supplies a reputation as one of the most progressive tile distributors in the UK - a reputation which the company intends to maintain, making sure the people of Coventry and beyond are well supplied with stylish tiles well into the next millennium.

Above: *The founders of the company.*
Top: *Edmund Road retail shop.*
Left: *Landrover have specified Capitol Tiles in all their showrooms.*

million. Today, it has ten retail outlets throughout the Midlands, in Nuneaton, Rugby, Wolverhampton, Kidderminster and Leamington Spa, and as far afield as Banbury and Oxford. The main warehouse has recently undergone a complete overhaul, and now benefits from high-level racking and modern warehouse management systems. Products stocked there include polished, unpolished and rectified (cut edge) porcelain, large format monocottura wall and floor tiles, one-price plains and decors, and speciality pieces for swimming pools, factories and

Building up local amenities

In 1936, when a fully furnished house cost just a few hundred pounds, Mr George William Deeley came to Coventry and set up his own construction company in Avon Street, Stoke. George Deeley was himself the son of a builder and had gained useful experience of the industry in his father's firm, and his new business, in its brief pre-war existence, was successful in securing various construction projects including a certain amount of council housing. But no sooner had the firm become nicely established than the outbreak of war disrupted everything; building activities were now directed towards repairs and first aid to damaged buildings in and around Coventry, and to supplement this work Deeley operated a small haulage company which transported, among other things, the materials needed for building aerodrome runways, and also provided a local coal delivery service. Government licensing permitted the construction of a very limited amount of new private housing towards the end of the war, but it was not until the war was over, and Coventry was left to survey the extent of damage it had sustained and assess what was needed, that rebuilding began in earnest.

Immediate priorities were housing for those who had been made homeless, and schools for the children. Most of G W Deeley's work at this time was commissioned by Coventry Corporation and the various Local Authorities. To begin with the bulk of the contracts awarded to the firm was for Local Authority council houses, and a labour force of some 30 men was built up to carry out this work; once the initial crisis had been overcome and council house building programmes slowed down, the company moved into the private sector and

Above: *One of G W Deeley's haulage fleet, a Bedford wagon used for transporting coal and material for building aerodrome runways during the second world war.* ***Below:*** *The Head Office at Torrington Avenue, shortly after the Company first moved there in the early 1950s.*

continued building on various parcels of land across the area. One of its largest developments was at Willenhall, where over 300 private houses were erected.

Schools were a new venture for Deeley, but as more and more School contracts came its way they became rather a speciality of the firm during the 1960s and 1970s.

In February 1948 a Limited Company was formed, under the name of G W Deeley Limited, with George Deeley and his wife as joint Directors. As work continued to flow in, the firm steadily expanded and by the end of the 1950s it had outgrown its Avon Street premises. A convenient plot of wasteland lay nearby, and the company put in an application to develop it, but planning permission was withheld. However, as the Local Authority, then as now, had a policy of encouraging local employment, it made an alternative offer of land in Torrington Avenue, available on lease. This was found acceptable, so Deeley's offices and builders' yard moved to Torrington Avenue, and the foundations were laid for the company's current headquarters.

Subsequent growth, including the acquisition of several existing businesses, enabled the company to extend its range of services, and to expand its operations over a wider geographical area, with offices in Northampton and Aylesbury as well as Coventry. Overseas markets were also investigated, and for a while during the 1970s and early 80s the company operated an international subsidiary based in Saudi Arabia; this proved a relatively short-lived venture but one which gave the firm invaluable experience.

As the company grew in both size and reputation, it became involved with an increasingly varied range of contracts which included many industrial and municipal building projects. In the interests of flexibility, a rationalised structure of divisions and subsidiaries was established. Areas of operation were steadily expanded and licences were negotiated for the use and distribution of patented building systems. The company now offers specialised expertise in fitting-out, redesign and refurbishment and Design and Build, complementing its original construction and civil engineering skills, and over the years has been involved in some interesting projects.

Construction projects have included the Head Office of Jaguar Cars in Coventry, the UK headquarters of Hallmark Cards at Henley-on-Thames, a high bay container warehouse for Robinsons Removals in Aylesbury, Buckinghamshire, and the Eastern

> **"AS WORK CONTINUED TO FLOW IN, THE FIRM STEADILY EXPANDED AND BY THE END OF THE 1950S IT HAD OUTGROWN ITS AVON STREET PREMISES"**

*Left: Phase one of Coventry Technical College, 1936. **Below:** Phase 6 of Coventry Technical College, completed in 1979.*

Perimeter Road at Bicester. Jaguar Cars also commissioned Deeley to undertake the fitting-out of their impressive museum and theatre, and other clients for whom the company has undertaken fitting-out projects have included Boots the Chemists and the De Vere Hotel in Coventry, and the Powergen Headquarters in Birmingham.

In the area of Redesign and Refurbishment, Deeley has the resources to meet the needs of a wide range of clients, and is equipped to undertake projects of any size and type, from factories to listed buildings. Deeley provides a dedicated team which works in close partnership with the client throughout the project, from inception to completion; concept and budgetary constraints are often an important factor in projects of this nature, and a high level of site control is exercised as this is often a critical factor in ensuring that the client's cost, quality and time objectives are met. Examples of redesign and refurbishment projects can be seen in Coventry at Sandvik and Brose, and further afield, at Nuneaton, Deeley was responsible for revitalising Bermuda Village.

Design and Build has become the fastest-growing method of commissioning new buildings. It is an extremely cost-effective and time-efficient means of construction. Deeley is one of the pioneers of this method in the UK, offering a Total Concept service that covers all aspects of a project. This can include everything from the preliminaries - operational research, locating a site, finance and feasibility studies, planning and building regulations consents - through the construction process, to the handover of the completed facility, and beyond.

One of the company's Design and Build projects which will be familiar to most Coventry residents is the Central Six Retail Park, a 144000 square foot fashion retail park near Coventry city centre, undertaken in partnership with Boots Properties plc. The thirteen-acre site to be developed was a contaminated railway yard adjacent to Coventry Central Railway Station, and substantial ground stabilisation was required. The brief was to produce a design of traditional appearance; spacious arcades were specified by the client, to enable customers to move between shop units, and the development was required to meet traditional institutional standards. Extensive consultations were held with Coventry City Council in connection with the planning application

Top: This building was originally built for Standard Motor Company in 1936 as a Shadow Aero Engine factory and is now occupied by Massey Ferguson Manufacturing Ltd.
Above: *Mr Peter Deeley, current Chairman of Deeley Group Limited.*

and the substantial offsite infrastructure requirements; a new access roundabout was planned, major retaining walls were to be constructed, and a key feature of the project was a 90 metre long suspension footbridge which links the suburb of Earlsdon with the City Centre, across the adjacent railway tracks and into the site. A 1000 space car park was provided, and fourteen units ranging in size from 800 to 2000 square metres were prepared ready for tenants to fit out. The whole of the front facade faces south so that natural light can be used to maximum effect, and the whole development is designed so as to blend in with, rather than dominate, its residential surroundings. The scheme also provided for extensive landscaping works including the planting of indigenous species. Throughout, Deeley worked closely with Boots Properties and other interested parties, and successfully achieved the desired result within the contract deadline. Construction was in fact completed within the impressive timescale of 36 weeks.

One of the Company's fundamental principals is that all development should contribute to improving standards and amenities for the whole community, and aesthetic and environmental considerations are of prime importance. This, combined with its high standards of workmanship, its flexible approach, its ability to work as part of a team and its success in achieving set objectives, has ensured a very high level of repeat business. With an extensive client list which includes many local, national and international companies, public bodies, community, health and educational organisations, housing associations, religious groups, research bodies, Development Corporations, local government and Government agencies, Deeley's achievements can be seen throughout the Midlands and beyond, from Holiday Inns' laundry facility in London to the Budgen Foodstore in Holt, Norfolk, and from Marks and Spencer in Leicester to Massey-Ferguson in Banner Lane Coventry and to BCWA's headquarters in Bristol. Projects for clients in the leisure industry include AT7 Leisure and AMF Bowl in Coventry, and Northampton RFC's stadium; projects for the public sector include the King Henry VIII School in Coventry, Coventry Technical College, and work for the Midland Aircraft Museum Trust at Coventry Airport; while residential properties range from first-time buyer homes to individually designed executive houses.

The current Chairman of the Company is Mr Peter Deeley, son of the founder. Peter Deeley attaches great importance to the value of the local community; he is firmly committed to investing in the local economy, and has promoted the Company's active interest in youth training and the disabled, and its involvement with the Midlands Sports Centre for the Disabled at Tile Hill. Throughout its expansion and growth, the firm has remained at heart very much a local business, and has maintained the important family atmosphere on which the whole venture was founded so many years ago.

*Below: Directors of G W Deeley Limited, from left to right: Vince Free, Peter Goodgame, Mike Johnson, Clive Rattenbury, Peter Deeley and Brian Crawford. **Bottom left:** One of Deeley Group's most recent projects in Coventry, the Central Six Retail Park.*

Success on a plate

In 1957 the BBC and a national newspaper jointly sponsored a competition for enterprising businessmen entitled 'Be Your Own Boss'. Amongst the entrants was Richard Naylor, a Yorkshireman living in Coventry. A former employee of the GEC Applied Electronics Company at Browns Lane, Coventry, Richard was not only highly qualified, having studied to postgraduate level, but also had a flair for business and a particular interest in the future markets for high quality precious metal finishes which he foresaw would soon open up in the rapidly-developing electronics and telecommunications industries. The judges of the competition awarded the prize of £3,500 to Richard, and posterity has confirmed the soundness of their choice. The prize money was used to fund the establishment of Precious Metal Depositors Limited, and in the 40-plus years since that time the company has gone from strength to strength to become the PMD Group, carrying out million-pound contracts in China, India and the USA.

Prior to the establishment of PMD, Richard had in 1955 formed a partnership with another former GEC employee, Eddie Marlow. Richard and Eddie had both been involved at GEC in the early experimental work on printed and potted circuit boards, and in the electroforming of wave guides for the Sea Slug Guidance System; Eddie had worked in the metal finishing department, and Richard in the laboratories. When GEC had announced its intention to relocate to Portsmouth, neither Richard nor Eddie wanted to leave Coventry, and they discussed the options open to them.

Between them they had all the skills and experience necessary to provide a specialised precious metal coating service; and they were confident of the existence of a niche market for such a service. Apart from themselves, the only people who carried out precious metal plating at that time were the jewellery

Top left: *Richard Naylor, co-founder of the Company.*
Right: *Eddie Marlow, co-founder of the Company.*
Below: *The original Company premises on Hearsall Lane.*

advantage: they were still bound by the Official Secrets Act from their days at GEC. This meant that they could continue processing GEC components, subject to control by the Aircraft Inspection Department; they subsequently applied for Departmental approval in their own right, and this was granted, opening up new avenues for the company.

Employing a workforce of seven, they moved to new premises at Hearsall Lane, Coventry, where they eagerly carried out plating work of any description - they silver-plated car reflectors, they stripped and gold-plated watch cases, and they replated household items such as teapots, and meanwhile they continued their research while they waited for the electronics industry to grow.

manufacturers, and standards of purity required by the jewellery industry were very different from those required by the electronics industry; for jewellery use it was sufficient to simply dip items into a bowl of gold solution over a gas fire. However, the manufacturers of electronic components required gold deposits of a much more rigorous degree of purity.

So Richard and Eddie each put £2-12s-6d into their new business venture as capital, and rented premises at Warwick Row, Coventry. Whilst they had the requisite skills and experience, they still needed equipment, and funds were short. So ordinary domestic items bought from the local stores acted as containers for the electroplating solutions, and Richard and Eddie assembled the equipment they needed themselves, building rectifiers and electrical gadgets by hand from spare components. Their main outlay was on the precious metals they used.

Richard proved adept at generating business, approaching buyers in the electronics industry personally and outlining the concept of the new venture - a rigorously-controlled bespoke plating company aimed specifically at the electronics market and associated aerospace industry. Their innovative approach and the high-quality finishes which they created soon brought them to the attention of trade buyers. Early jobs tended to be in small batches, and were typically the more technically difficult projects that customers found difficult to get processed elsewhere. As recognition of the new enterprise became more widespread, and trade buyers began to place their confidence in Richard and Eddie's technical ability, the business grew rapidly.

Besides Richard's business acumen and Eddie's technical expertise, the partnership had another

*Top left: The High Altar Cross in Coventry Cathedral, plated by PMD. **Below:** Arsenal's Charlie George and Richard Naylor with the Golden Goal Trophy plated by PMD.*

projects, including the early British aerospace programme where it provided the finish on the outer skins of the satellites and a number of other components.

An important innovation was the development of the technique of through-hole plating of electronic circuit boards using copper as the undercoating conductor metal instead of silver, which had previously been used. Copper proved both less expensive and more satisfactory, and this technique became the accepted method worldwide.

All this happened in the two years before Richard's success in the 'Be Your Own Boss' competition. With the £3,500 prize money he was able to set up Precious Metal Depositors, where he became Managing Director with Eddie as Technical Director. With capital behind it, the company made a profit of £300 - its first profit. The electronics industry was now providing them with a steady supply of work, and they were plating some 250,000 small electronic components a month through conventional plating tanks. The introduction of the reel-to-reel method of plating, a conveyor-belt system which combined speed with precision, increased throughput dramatically to up to 15 million components a month. This plating method, pioneered by Richard and Eddie, revolutionised the plating process, rendering other systems obsolete virtually overnight, and it is this method which is still used today.

As Richard had predicted, the rapid expansion of the electronics industry continued and its applications within telecommunications, computing and aerospace continued to multiply. Precious Metal Depositors was involved with many exciting and pioneering

Encouraged by their success, Richard and Eddie extended their activities into the supply of chemical processes for finishing and started a sister company, PMD Chemicals Limited. This company offered an advisory service and pioneered new plating materials to meet specific applications within the semiconductor and transistor industries; for instance, a range of gold solutions low in free cyanide and nearly neutral in pH value was developed for gold-plating circuits without attacking resists, adhesives or laminate. A treatment to prevent corrosion of aluminium surfaces was also developed and patented.

Top left: An interior view of PMD's premises. *Top right:* Coated circuit boards. *Below:* Another interior aspect of the Company's factory.

Subsequently an engineering division, PMD Engineering, was created, originally to design and build small items of equipment needed by the precious metal plating industry such as rectifiers and amp-hour meters, and going on to design, manufacture and install electroplating and surface treatment equipment for a range of customers.

In 1960, to cope with increasing demand, a bespoke factory was designed by local architects Helberg and built at Broad Lane, Coventry. Also in that year, PMD was the centre of a great deal of media attention when Eddie Marlow and a colleague carried out the gold-plating of an altar cross and two candlesticks for the inauguration of Coventry Cathedral.

PMD's expansion continued with the launch of PMD Continentale in Brussels, which supplied chemical processes to customers in the electronics industry, in Belgium, the Netherlands, Luxembourg and France. PMD's development team continued at the forefront of surface treatment technology, constantly building upon its existing expertise to develop new plating techniques, new chemical processes and innovative answers to processing problems. One novel application was the ability to plate on non-conductive surfaces which in 1971 led to the Golden Boot, a gold plated leather football boot which was awarded to the scorer of the winning goal in

the FA Cup Final. Although this award ceased in 1977 a special one-off was presented in 1987 when Coventry City FC won the FA Cup.

PMD continued to grow to such an extent that the factory at Broad Lane had to be extended in 1965, an exercise that was repeated in 1969, 1971 and 1977. At the age of 53, Richard Naylor died after a long battle against cancer. The following year, 1984, the Group expanded by acquiring Metallic Protectives Ltd of Warwick thus adding further surface treatment capabilities to its portfolio.

Richard's son Mark Naylor, who had joined Precious Metal Depositors in 1980, took control of the Group in 1989 at a time of severe recession in the electronics industry. To survive this recession PMD (UK) Ltd was born out of the combination of Precious Metal Depositors Ltd and PMD Chemicals Ltd.

Under Mark Naylor's leadership the Group emerged from the recession and again started to grow, which again exerted pressure on the space available at Broad Lane. In 1996 a £1 million refurbishment project was started which would be the final development of the Broad Lane site.

The company, which Richard and Eddie founded and which owes so much to the sheer brilliance of these two men, remains as committed as ever to innovation and improvement and continues to make a contribution to the global electronics industry.

*Top left: Reel to reel plating. **Right:** The current Managing Director Mark Naylor. **Below:** The Company's current premises.*

Fun, thrills, and entertainment from the heart

A young and talented actor named Brian Reece helped to write history when he played the leading role as Jack Worthing in the British première of 'Half In Earnest', a musical version of 'The Importance Of Being Earnest'. The date was 27th March 1958, and the musical was Coventry's brand new Belgrade Theatre's very first production. The Belgrade was Britain's first theatre to be built after the second world war, and it was particularly significant that its location was Coventry, one of the cities left in ruins by Nazi bombs.

The theatre was officially opened by the Duchess of Kent, who paid tribute to the courage and vision of those who had planned and built the city anew, an achievement crowned by the 'bold and imaginative enterprise' that had created The Belgrade.

Since 1946 repertory theatre had been kept alive in the city by the Midland Theatre Company, but Coventry Council had long seen the need for a new theatre and in 1955 city councillors gave the go-ahead to a scheme for a civic theatre to be built on land in Corporation Street. At a cost of £300,000 - around one pound a head of the population - the construction work got underway. The building's steel framework quickly went up and from there the new theatre grew rapidly. There was little mechanical help, and the ambitious project required 150 manual workers. In less than two years it was ready for the all-important finishing touches. The stage was painstakingly sanded, floorings and furnishings added, and artist Martin Froy designed a mosaic mural based on a four seasons theme for the rear walls of the foyers.

A generous gift of gleaming Yugoslavian beech from Coventry's twin city, Belgrade, enhanced some of the ceilings and the sound reflectors over the proscenium opening. Up to that time no name had been given to the new theatre, so in recognition of the gift it was decided to name the building The Belgrade Theatre. A sculptured concrete panel based on a 17th century engraving symbolising the city of Belgrade was mounted over the theatre's main entrance.

If the organisers had any doubts about the theatre's success, they need not have worried. The opening night was a glittering occasion attended by the Mayor Pearl Hyde and all the civic dignitaries; Princess Marina, smiling and vibrant in a wine-coloured full-length evening gown, occupied the royal box.

From that very first memorable production The Belgrade's successful future was assured. With tickets available from half a crown ($12^1/_2$ pence) to seven and sixpence ($37^1/_2$ pence), an evening at the theatre was within the reach of most pockets - even senior citizens, who were able to attend Thursday matinees for only a shilling.

1963 saw The Belgrade pioneering an exciting new project, Theatre in Education. The theatre still offers a wide range of workshops and activities that school children can get involved in, with special rates offered for school parties.

Many actors who later found stardom began their careers at The Belgrade: Michael Crawford, who later made his mark as the inept and blundering Frank Spencer in 'Some Mothers do Have 'em' - and

Top right: *A 1960s view of the Belgrade Theatre.*
Left: *Clare Humphrey and Robert Bladen on stage in October 1998 in 'It's a Lovely Day Tomorrow' - a play about Coventry during the Blitz.*

Ian Tilton

Ian Tilton

went on to delight audiences with his outstanding abilities as a serious actor; Richard Briers, who became one of Britain's most popular comedy actors, and Bill Owen, whose early roles bore no resemblance to Compo, the moth-eaten character who made him a household name.

Over the years many famous feet have trodden the boards of The Belgrade Theatre in productions that range from Shakespeare to pantomime. The brilliance of performers like Susannah York, Richard Todd and Bert Kwouk, and the comic talents of Frankie Howerd, Billy Dainty, Barbara Windsor and Ken Dodd have become legendary in the theatre's history. Who among the audience can forget the many faces of David Suchet, who competently played three parts in 'Arsenic and Old Lace' in 1972, or Timothy Dalton's outstanding performance in Peter Shaffer's 'The Royal Hunt of the Sun' in 1970?

Today's productions are no less exciting, from imaginative comedies and traditional dramas to rock 'n roll musicals. September 1996 saw the beginning of a pioneering new venture - the Singles Night. The special evenings staged for single people who share a common love of the theatre proved to be immensely popular, and form an ongoing part of The Belgrade's programme. Not slow to take advantage of new technology, The Belgrade Theatre got itself a website in 1996 for the benefit of theatre-goers surfing the net. The site has up-to-the-minute news as well as programme and ticket information. From Spring 1999 it will be possible to purchase tickets through the site, making The Belgrade the first theatre in the country to offer the service.

Above: *A scene from 'The Wedding', May 1998.*

The Belgrade's current Director Bob Eaton once said, 'We want to provide something really exciting for theatre-goers to enjoy.' The Theatre now prides itself on having achieved a close relationship with its customers and audiences in putting together a wide ranging programme of theatre for all. As we approach the Millennium the theatre-goers of Coventry would agree that many more of those sparkling occasions lie ahead of the theatre that has kept them brilliantly entertained so far.

12,000 affordable Touchstone Homes

The political dream of a home owning democracy is still a dream for many who are ineligible for, let alone able to take out, the mortgages by which Mr and Mrs Average buy their homes. Those on low wages, unemployed or on minimal pensions face council house waiting lists or private rentals from employers or independent landlords and housing associations. While many are well content with the homes they rent there are still those trapped in situations exposed in the mid-60s by the shocking drama-documentary 'Cathy Come Home'.

At that time the local paper gave considerable coverage to a new organisation, the Coventry Churches Housing Association, pledged to provide decent affordable housing to those in need. From the small beginnings of a few refurbished old houses in Coventry has grown the Touchstone Housing Association (1994) covering the urban West Midlands. The emphasis is still that of Christian charity in its less understood sense of love your neighbours by treating them as you, yourself, would wish to be treated.

In order to achieve these aims in the latter half of the 20th century it is necessary to run an effective business in making money work to provide results. The five Touchstone teams cooperate to improve the quality of care, homes and servicing for all its customers. Sound financial management is of the essence in enabling the Housing Association to bridge the gap between renting and buying by securing tax reliefs shared with Touchstone customers. To 1200 households a year such schemes provide the only opportunity to acquire a home where they can enjoy peace of mind.

Through the Touchline telecall centre those in need are provided with advice pertaining to money management, social security entitlements and most importantly an immediate answer to the question 'Can you house me?' Touchstone tenants are provided with maintenance services which many a hard pressed council would envy. In keeping with the founders' beliefs that people who take responsibility for their homes also take a pride in caring for them is the Touchstone policy of devolving management of local residents' groups to the tenants themselves.

Top right: *Regenerating urban communities.* ***Above right:*** *Bill Martin, Chief Executive of Touchstone Housing Association.* ***Left:*** *Richard Farnell, Chairman, presenting Hildegard Atherton (retiring board member and co-founder of Coventry Churches Housing Association) with a bouquet and commemorative book and making her Honorary Life President.*

Stepping out in style

It was 1840 when the name Charles Ager first appeared above a small shop in West Orchard. Inside the shop, Charles and his wife Mary sold and repaired boots, soon building up a reputation for high quality workmanship. Mary was the daughter of a Warwickshire yeoman farmer, and Charles, son of a farming family from the little Northampton village of Irthlingborough, had come to Coventry in the 1820s and learnt the craft of bootmaking from a cobbler named Piggot in High Street.

The success of the business lies in the exceptional craftsmanship of every item made. From the sturdy boots which Charles's original customers needed, to the lighter-weight footwear which was in demand when cycling came into vogue, and even skating boots, successive Agers combined a progressive outlook with good workmanship. For instance, the founder's grandson Charles John Ager - who got many ideas from specially imported American trade papers and was one of the first traders in Coventry to use name-printed bags - was quick to respond to the demand for coloured leathers and lighter footwear when the reduced number of horses in the streets made the wearing of lighter footwear possible. He also had an X-ray machine, which, together with his electric cash-register which was

one of the first outside London, made his shop a great centre of interest for shoppers, and Agers was regarded as the most up-market shoe retailer in the city.

To this day, Ager is known throughout Coventry and beyond for its quality stock and personal attention. In spite of increasing competition from other footwear outlets in the re-developed city, Ager has been able to continue trading successfully in high quality shoes, with a current turnover of some 25,000 pairs annually.

Agers is the largest retailer of Clarks children's shoes in the Midlands, and is staffed by trained shoe fitters with many years' experience, especially in fitting children's footwear. It is the firm's policy to provide the public with the highest possible standard of service and choice, offering their customers a superior range of footwear not available in modern shopping precincts.

And the foreseeable future of this family business . . . that lies is in the hands of Christopher Ager Hart, who joined his parents in 1989, as the sixth generation of the Coventry footwear dynasty.

Top left: *Company founder, Charles Ager.* ***Left:*** *The imposing facade of the shop on Smithford Street in 1860.* ***Above:*** *Charles and Ivan survey the remains of the Smithford Street shop following the Blitz in November 1940.*

The Society graced by Lady Godiva

An Englishman's home, as we all know, is his castle; it is also, in most cases, the largest investment he makes during his lifetime; and more often than not, it is bought with a mortgage. Today, thanks to the wide range of advice and services offered by building societies such as the Coventry, it is relatively easy to become a homeowner. During the industrial revolution, however, acquiring decent housing posed a problem for the workers who had left their traditional homes in farming communities to come to work in the new industries in towns and cities. There was no state provision for housing; some employers were able to offer living accommodation, and industrial benefactors such as Cadburys who provided model housing estates were assured of a queue of applicants for jobs and a loyal, long-serving workforce. Overall, however, there was a serious lack of suitable accommodation for workers and their families. Friendly Societies already existed, providing a range of benefits to subscribing members, and in response to the need for housing a new form of friendly society was created: the building society. Members clubbed together and paid monthly subscriptions, and as funds became available the societies bought land; when building commenced, members carried out as much work themselves as their combined skills and time permitted. As each house was completed, a ballot of members was held and the winner moved into the house; however, everybody carried on paying their monthly subscription until all the members had been housed, and not until then would home ownership be transferred from the society to individual members. Finally, any remaining funds were shared out and the society, having fulfilled its purpose, would close.

The first recorded building society was formed in Birmingham in 1775. Practices and procedures were modified and refined over the years; the ballot system, for instance, was abolished by the Building Societies Act of 1894. During the 19th century societies began to accept investments from members seeking a financial return on their money rather than home ownership, and 'permanent' building societies, offering home loans and savings facilities, became established.

The Coventry Permanent Economic Building Society was founded in February 1884 by a small group of citizens, one of whom was Thomas Mason Daffern, a man of exceptional gifts who became the Society's first Secretary, and to whom the Society is indebted for the high standards of integrity and independence which he exercised in his involvement with its affairs over a period of almost half a century. Thomas Daffern and his associates gathered in the Coventry Institute and contributed anything from a tanner (6d or 2.5p) to half a crown (2/6d or 12.5p) each, raising a fund totalling £1 2s 6d, at a time when Coventry's economy was stagnating due to the decline of the city's traditional industries of silk weaving and watch-making.

Coventry citizens have a long tradition of bravery in the face of economic challenge. The courageous stand taken by these founder members, and the concern with which the Coventry Building Society has, from that moment on, protected the financial interests of its members, parallels Lady Godiva's courage in fulfilling her part of a bargain with her husband; Earl Leofric had agreed to waive additional taxes on his wife's fellow citizens if she rode naked through Coventry. It is in recognition of this that in the early 1970s the Society adopted its famous 'Lady Godiva' logo.

Top: *Thomas Mason Daffern, the Society's founder and first Secretary.* ***Right:*** *The High Street Office pictured in 1934.*

New industries came to Coventry in the late 19th century. Coventry-built bicycles enabled young men and women to enjoy unprecedented independence through the new vogue for cycling; and the developing motor industry, too, chose Coventry as its home. The electrical and chemical industries followed. Workers arrived in search of jobs. In the forty years up to 1911 the city's population doubled, creating a greatly increased demand for housing and mortgages; and as workers prospered, they had money to invest. By the beginning of the first world war, the 'Economic', as it was known, had become the largest society in the area in terms of assets, and many local families had begun an association with the Society as investors and borrowers which subsequent generations have been happy to preserve to this day.

A series of mergers in the 70s and 80s greatly enhanced the Society's assets, and in 1983, following a merger with the Coventry Provident, it was renamed the Coventry Building Society. Currently the seventh largest building society in the UK with assets of £5 billion and 50 branches, the Coventry Building Society is committed to offering tangible benefits to customers through competitively-priced products and excellent service standards, and is regularly featured in the financial press for 'best buy' mortgage and savings products. For well over a century the Coventry Building Society has been helping people achieve their dreams of become home owners. The many social and economic changes which have taken place during that period have resulted in building societies taking on a significantly different role from that of the early friendly and terminating societies. The legislation governing financial institutions, too, has undergone radical revision. However, the Coventry Building Society, led by a dedicated team of financial experts including Chief Executive Martin H Ritchley, who joined the Society in 1970 as Chief Accountant (having previously worked for the Society's auditors), will ensure that the Society continues to serve its members in the best and most appropriate way. The Society recorded an exceptional performance in 1998, and looks forward to an equally successful future in which more and more people will enjoy the combined benefits of home ownership, and membership of one of the most efficient building societies in the United Kingdom - the Coventry.

Left: An early example of the Society's advertising. *Right:* An illustration depicting Coventry's many trades and industries. *Below:* The original Sir William Reid Dick statue of Lady Godiva, now the Society's symbol.

Small, clean and efficient!

The Bartlett family's Sand, Gravel, Stone and Ashes haulage businesses are well advertised by their clean bright red and blue lorries. Clean lorries! In quarries! They're busy too! You may think this an unusual combination but it has always worked ever since the 24 year old Neil Bartlett, a Somerset man from Taunton, bought his first second hand truck in 1967. He'd been driving trucks for others since he was 17 and moved to Coventry to achieve his aim of being an owner/driver at a cost of £700. With the old Bedford TK went an existing haulage contract with one of the many quarries catering for the burgeoning motorway and housing building boom of the 60s and 70s. He operated from premises at Webster Street for five years.

Helped by his wife, Marie, he was soon ready to trade in the old TK and buy a new truck but the dealer was unwilling to take the old one as a trade in so he kept it and still had a good deal on the price of the new vehicle. Brother-in-law Ian joined as second driver and by 1973 they bought a new Leyland and took on their first employee at their new premises in Clovelly Road where the business was based until 1982.

It was the exhaustion of winnable resources that closed their main quarry client down and provided the opening for the young firm's expansion from haulier to merchant. Practically overnight Bartletts were tipped into business as a supplier of sand and gravel buying materials from the quarry operators for sale to builders in quantities too small for the quarry owners to consider using their own transport for deliveries. At the time Neil Bartlett regarded his overalls as his best suit preferring to continue as an owner/driver avoiding the pit-falls of over-fast expansion which have ruined many young businesses.

He found his niche in catering for trade which larger concerns regarded as non-cost efficient and is in the happy position of catering for them without competing against them. In the 1980s he would happily advise prospective clients wanting larger quantities than his norm to deal direct with the quarry companies. To his surprise he found British truck builders and dealers in the 1970s could not be bothered to visit his small firm but the Swedish company Volvo did. To this day his family runs Volvo vehicles.

His drivers are encouraged to keep their lorries clean during the week and to undertake a full weekly scrub and polish of paintwork and undercarriage to match the mechanical maintenance routine of the company workshops. Following their seven years average

Above: *One of Neil Bartlett's lorries in 1972.*
Below: *Drivers and their immaculate lorries line up in 1983, from left to right: Neil Bartlett, Alan Healey, Ian Bartlett (Neil's brother), Arthur Morris, Frank Boufy, Joe Bartlett (Neil's son) and Dick March.*

service with Bartletts the trucks are easily sold at
enhanced prices to others requiring vehicles in good
clean condition with a sound service record reflecting
the quality of both drivers and mechanics employed
by Bartletts.

Neil was one of the local pioneers of equipping his
vehicles with two way radios, those essential tools for
ensuring that no vehicle ever runs empty by missing a
nearby pick-up adjacent to their last drop-off. By
1982 he had moved to the present site at the former
Binley Pit which enjoys greatly increased storage
space. It was this that enabled Bartletts lorries to
travel loaded from their last quarry pick-ups, to off-
load and store the material to be on hand for the first
customer ordering it from stock.

Even better in that these facilities scotched the ploys
of a few clients who claimed that the wrong size or
grade of material had been delivered but that they
were willing to accept delivery at a reduced price.
Bartletts, with storage facilities at Exhall since 1998,
and their own loading shovel, no longer had to accept
such deals. The worldly wise will not be surprised that
such devious souls stopped playing games with a firm
holding a better hand of cards.

Today the family firm has a fleet of 25 lorries. This,
in accordance with the founder's firm belief in the
efficiency of small units, is shared between three

divisions. Neil Bartlett (Haulage) Ltd, is Dad's show,
and those run by his two sons are Joe's enterprise,
JJ Bartlett (Haulage) and Gary's outfit,
Gary J Bartlett & Son.

Above: *Neil and Marie Bartlett in front of some of
their fleet of 25 lorries.* **Below:** *An aerial view of the
Company's Exhall premises.*

The smoothest way to go

Thirty years ago, If a fortune-teller had told Mike de Courcey that a successful future lay ahead in the transport industry, he might have wondered whether she was referring to his job with Standard Triumph Cars or to his part-time coach-driving. The answer, of course, would have been neither. She would have been thinking of De Courcey Travel, the company which Mike set up in 1970, with one coach and one double-decker bus which he had bought out of his savings.

Mike's early contracts were for private hire work and school services; factory bus services soon became an important part of the business as well, although closures and reduction of Coventry's traditional works have reduced these to a point where only one works service is still operating. Mike has always concentrated on providing the services that local people need, giving them access to the places they want to visit for social, entertainment, educational and work purposes. For instance, he recently started a service between Rugby and Nuneaton, providing a direct link with Walsgrave Hospital, and this has not only made the two towns' facilities more accessible to each other, but also simplified the journey tremendously for those visiting friends and relatives at the hospital; previously they had to catch a bus to Coventry and change to another bus at Pool Meadow. The service has made it easier for students from either town to travel to the North Warwickshire and Rugby colleges, and many people are now able to spend an evening at the Showcase cinema without worrying about how to get back home afterwards. This, to Mike, is what the busi-

Above: *Mike de Courcey on one of his buses.*
Below: *A de Courcey executive coach outside Coventry Cathedral, one of the city's more famous landmarks.*

capacity. All the vehicles are in contact with base by radio or telephone, so that any unexpected situation which might arise can be quickly resolved. The fleet includes low-floor vehicles and coaches fitted with lifts, allowing easy access for the disabled, and over the years Mike has been very much involved in helping those with mobility difficulties.

The firm moved to its current purpose-built site in Rowley Drive, Coventry, in 1973, moving there from its original premises in Tile Hill. With its current management team of Mike de Courcey (MD), Bob Wildman (General Manager), Mick Malin (Operations Manager), Alex Miller (Bus Services Manager) and Tom O'Sullivan (Chief Engineer), the company believes in investment in people; staff are encouraged to undertake training for NVQ and Assessor and Verifier qualifications, and Mike de Courcey Travel Ltd is a BCT approved centre for driver training. Mike's wife Bernadette, who has been involved with the running of the business since before their marriage in 1976, is now Company Secretary. Plans for the future are simply to continue to operate to a high standard in the West Midlands and

ness is all about - 'We want to provide service,' he says, 'and we're here to help people.'

Warwickshire areas, and to expand gently in line with circumstances.

With 45 buses and coaches now in service - most of them easily identifiable by their personalised MJ number plates - Mike de Courcey Travel is the largest private coach and bus company in the West Midlands and Warwickshire, and has its own shop in the bus station where customers can find information about all the company's services. As well as operating daily services throughout rural Warwickshire and Coventry the company is the main private provider of school bus services in Coventry, carrying some 3,500 school children a day. The many local people who have enjoyed tours to various parts of the UK on Mike's luxury coaches or taken advantage of his regular shopping trips to Calais will be pleased to learn that the company has recently begun to offer tours to the Continent as well. Other services include conference shuttle services, transport to evening functions, sightseeing tours from a special open-topped bus, and private hire for special events. For large groups, midi-buses provide extra seating

Above: *A Godiva Sightseeing Tour open top bus. The service was launched in 1995.* ***Below:*** *Mike de Courcey, second right, ordering new Marshal SLF Buses at the Coach and Bus Show at the National Exhibition Centre in 1997.*

Nearly 270 years of burning legal issues in Coventry

In 1980, Coventry firm of solicitors Seymour, Smith and Co celebrated its 250th anniversary. One of the events held to mark the occasion was a lunch given by Sun Alliance in the crypt of St Mary's Hall, Coventry, and after the lunch Seymour Smith presented a very special and significant gift to Sun Alliance. The gift was a 'fire mark', the symbol, made of lead, which showed that a certain house was insured through a certain fire company. This particular fire mark dates from 1770 and was one of those issued by Sun Fire to its policyholders, and even still bore the policy number, clearly legible. Companies such as Sun Fire had their own fire brigades who would go out to fires when the alarm was raised and look to see if one of their marks was displayed on the premises. If it was, they would deal with the fire; if it was not, they would leave it.

In presenting this historic and valuable Sun fire mark to Sun Alliance, Seymour Smith was making reference back to its origins in 1730 when solicitor James Leigh became the Coventry agent for Sun Fire. The agency was carried on by James Leigh's successors; records show that at various times it was known as Dewes and Son, then Dewes, Son and Wilkes, then Arthur Seymour, then A and G Seymour, then, in the late 1920s, Seymour Smith and Co. James Leigh's original premises were in Hay Lane, Coventry, from where the firm moved to offices in Priory Street which were destroyed during the Blitz; many old documents were saved, fortunately, and now rest with the City Archivist. The firm's next premises were at Grosvenor Road,

Top left: Harry Smith. **Right:** *Fireman remove slates from the damaged roof of Seymour Smith's premises in October 1965.*

followed by a spell at 7 Queen Victoria Road before moving to their present offices at Queen's House, Queen's Road.

It was while they were at Queen Victoria Road, in 1965, that they had occasion to make a first-hand comparison between the services of today's fire brigade and the service which they themselves had represented some 235 years earlier. Today's fire brigade acquitted themselves well; the alarm call was received at 3.15 am, and within half an hour the blaze at Seymour Smith's premises had been brought under control. Detectives investigating the cause of the fire concluded that an intruder had entered the premises and had been using matches to look around, dropping them on the carpet when they burnt down; these matches had then started the fire. Some damage to the roof and third floor resulted, but fortunately no valuable documents were lost and Seymour Smith were able to reassure their clients that all deeds were undamaged.

Over the years successive incumbents of the practice have held many distinguished local posts, which include being the first Chapter Clerk to the Cathedral, the first Clerk of Meriden Rural District Council, Clerk to the Drapers', Mercers' and Clothiers' Companies, Clerk to the St Michael's Consolidated Charity and Head Office solicitors to the Coventry Building Society. Former senior partner Mr Ian Smith, a third generation Freeman of the City of Coventry has been for many years a director of the Coventry Building Society, has held such prestigious posts as Chairman of the Board of the Coventry Building Society and President of the Warwickshire Law Society, and is still attending the

office on a regular basis as a Consultant. Many of the firm's clients may also recall Mr Harry Smith, another former Senior Partner, his partners George Bancroft, Harry Clarke and Ronald Crompton and Mr Robert Baker and Mr Alfred Thornton, former senior legal executives who began as office boys and worked for the firm for more than 50 years.

The legal world has seen many changes during the lifetime of this exceptional firm. One change which springs to mind immediately is house prices; from 1929 to 1939 the price of an average house remained unchanged at £600, with a £100 Government subsidy, and all that was needed was a £50 deposit, although in fact many people paid cash, rather than take out a mortgage. Finding somewhere to live has become immeasurably more complex since then, but fortunately this firm offers a full range of domestic and conveyancing services and advice on leases and tenancy agreements to ensure that their clients' best interests are protected in all circumstances. It also handles wills, trusts and probates and accident and personal injury claims, and gives advice and assistance on employment matters, civil litigation, divorce and matrimonial issues, as well as providing a full service for business clients.

Seymour Smith and Co now practices in amalgamation with two other Coventry legal firms, Box and Sharpe, which was established by Ronald Box in 1959 in partnership with Gerald Sharpe, a former

Consultant with the firm and Roland Hollick and Co. founded in Coventry by Roland Hollick in 1910. From modern Queen's House premises, the company of Seymours (as it is now known), offers a comprehensive and specialised range of advice to individual and corporate clients, and is ideally placed to handle TransAction, the Law Society's National Conveyancing Protocol Scheme which is designed not only to speed up the conveyancing transaction but also to improve the efficiency of the service lawyers give to the public. With its up-to-date facilities and high professional standards, the firm looks forward to the burning legal challenges which the next 270 years might bring.

Top: Mr Ian Smith presents an historic fire mark to Mr Bob Gadd, left, an assistant general manager of Sun Alliance and Mr Ron Carley, Coventry Branch Manager.
Right: Mr Adrian Blay, the firm's Senior Partner.

The firm that always has the right solution

Binley Industrial Park is home to a chemical manufacturing firm which has had a tremendous impact on the lives of most people alive today; yet relatively few people have ever even heard of the company whose innovation, dedicated research and hard work has made it possible for them to hold a calculator in the palm of their hand, pack a laptop into their briefcase, or buy electronic equipment containing printed circuit boards (PCBs) at a fraction of the price they would have had to pay a few years ago.

Shipley first came to Coventry in the 1960s, setting up its headquarters in the former fire station near the aerodrome at Baginton. The parent company had been started in 1957 by an American couple, Charles and Lucia Shipley from Massachusetts, who ran a small chemical business from their garage and marketed their products to customers as far afield as the American mid-West. Their market soon expanded, however, they found distributors in France, Belgium, Germany, Austria, Holland, Switzerland, Italy and Scandinavia, while Coventry company PMD - also, coincidentally, founded in 1957 - began to distribute Shipley's products in the UK. It was as a result of this association with PMD that Shipley set up its first international subsidiary, Shipley Europe Limited, in Coventry.

The new company worked exclusively on the development of speciality chemicals for applications within the recently established, fast-developing electronics industry, supplying the ever-increasing number of PCB manufacturers in the south of England. By 1968

subsidiary sales companies had been established in Europe, and the premises at Baginton were no longer large enough; new manufacturing facilities were established on the former site of Smith's Stamping Works - which very conveniently came complete with the letter 'S' inlaid into the marble floor of the reception area. However, within a decade that site, too, had been outgrown, and the company had moved to its current site at Binley. In fact, Shipley was the first company to acquire land on the new industrial park, thus influencing the future development of the area and making it one of the most prestigious industrial developments in Coventry.

Below: *The premises in the 1960s.*
Bottom: *Early development of speciality chemicals.*

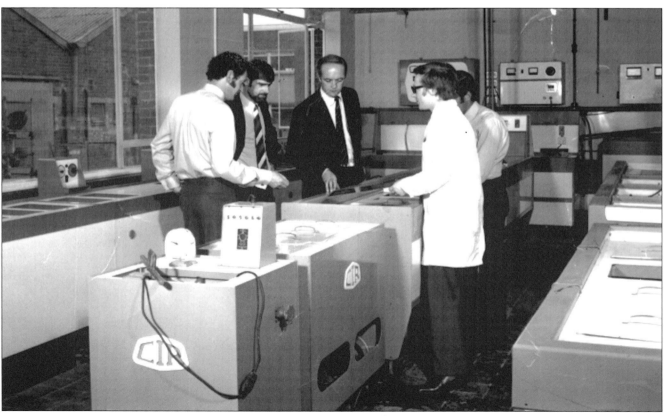

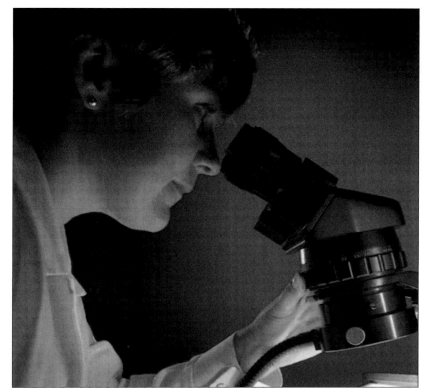

which produce the microscopic circuitry on silicon chips. As chips became smaller and faster, Shipley continued to innovate until now their chemicals can be used to produce lines less than one ten thousandth of a millimetre wide.

Shipley also developed chemistry to make copper adhere to printed circuit substrates, and this additive technology is used to put down copper onto printed circuits only where it is needed. There is therefore far less copper waste, making for a more environmentally friendly process as well as reducing manufacturing costs and therefore cost to the end user. Further environmental improvement was brought about by the introduction of 'Crimson', a process which avoided the use of copper at all in preparing substrates for electro-plating.

A world leader in supplying speciality chemical processes for PCBs and semi-conductor microlithography, Shipley attributes its success to the painstaking research and development work performed by its high calibre, hardworking workforce. Paradoxically, the little company which was at the forefront of miniaturisation has itself grown into a global business empire employing well over a thousand people. But the family-feel has been retained because every single employee is a valued member of the company, and is treated as such, sharing in the successes of the firm and working together to lead the microelectronics industry forward into the future.

This location has since proved ideal for a number of reasons, offering scope for expansion - the European Technical Centre has been established in adjoining units, and purchase of adjacent land has permitted the construction of purpose-built specialist facilities including a photo resist blending and packaging facility incorporating a Class 10 clean room.

Shipley is committed to environmental care; the company has sophisticated recycling and waste treat-ment plants and a team of fully trained emergency personnel standing by at all times. It has gained ISO9001 and 9002 certification and is currently pursuing accreditation to ISO14001 which encourages continuous environmental improvements. A new waste treatment plant has recently been commissioned at a total cost of £1 million.

The company has been responsible for a number of chemical innovations which have revolutionised the elec-tronics industry. For instance, the invention of Catalyst 6F, an agent that allows copper to be deposited on the inside of holes on printed circuit boards, meant that both sides of the board could be used, which in turn meant that the size of a PCB could be halved. As the microchip industry devel-oped, Shipley invented photo resists, chemicals

Above: A modern-day scientific process.
Below: Today's site at Binley Industrial Park.

The power of Reason

What happens when a professional speedway rider marries a go-ahead girl with experience in transport management? They start their own haulage business, of course; and that is exactly what John and Joan Reason did, back in the early 1950s. John had had a successful career in speedway, riding for the Coventry Bees and representing England on many occasions, and Joan, whose family owned Bantam Coaches, H & M Transport, LE Appleford Ltd, H J Partridge & Co with depots in Liverpool and Tower Bridge, London and was possibly the last company to be nationalised in the area, knew a great deal about the haulage industry. Operating from premises in East Street, Coventry and at Birchley Farm near Coombe Abbey, the young couple set about building up their business.

From the outset they adopted a flexible approach, taking the trouble to study their customers' needs and then working out the best and quickest way to respond to them. This, as they discovered, is an on-going process, as only through constant re-evaluation can they ensure that their services continue to match the changing needs and expectation of their customers. Customers tend to want bigger loads and faster turnaround; so, over the years, they have acquired more vehicles and expanded storage

and warehousing space. Keeping pace with new technology, the company uses a modern mobile communication system and its operations are supported by computerised logistics support.

Staff training is provided to ensure that all relevant industry standards are met; for example, the workforce includes a number of drivers who are HAZPAK qualified to carry chemicals and waste materials, and, as a British Standard ISO 9002 accredited company, its procedures are constantly monitored and reviewed to ensure that the firm's commitment to quality is reflected in all its working practices.

The fact that 80% of its business comes from clients who have used its services for over five years is clear proof that the company is continuing to meet its customers' needs. In fact, many have been customers for more than 20 years. Flexible as ever, the company has a policy that no job is too small and almost none too big; clients come from all sectors of business, industry and commerce, and include local, national and international companies of all sizes. Not surprisingly for a Coventry-based firm, more than 50% of Reasons' turnover is engineering-related, involving motor companies, tool makers, forges, driveshaft manufacturers and shopfitting companies. The company distributes cutting machinery to coal faces, carries new tractors and other items for the agricultural

Below: *Robert Reason, one of the family.*

British goods bound for the Continent, collected and warehoused by Reasons.

J & J Reason's current premises on the Binley Industrial Estate were purpose built in the early 1980s, together with 12 other industrial units by their own in-house building company, and a depot on Bodmin Road was opened in 1995; today, the company has a total of over 40,000 square feet of warehousing available at three depots situated within 15 miles of each other. Their fleet of vehicles ranges from small vans for the express delivery by courier of parcels all over the UK, to articulated lorries carrying 38 tonnes, and includes flatbeds and curtain-siders; all drivers are uniformed and equipped with mobile telephones to keep them in 24 hour communication with base and with each other;

sector, and delivers to motor manufacturers including Rover, Land Rover, Jaguar, Peugeot, and also to Honda at Swindon. For this sector that Reasons operates a sophisticated schedule of precisely timed deliveries; a manufacturer may, for instance, ask for a delivery every 18 minutes, to supply the production line. A steady supply of materials is crucial to the smooth running of the client's operation; the vehicle must arrive no more than five minutes early and definitely no more than one minute late. In practice, the drivers find it advisable to arrive in the vicinity in good time and wait a short distance away, so that they can turn up at the customer's premises exactly on time.

Continental traffic for the motor and other industries is handled in partnership with a firm of French hauliers which despatches a vehicle to Reasons' warehouse carrying goods from the Continent, for local distribution by Reasons; the same vehicle returns with a backload of

and to ensure that the fleet expertly maintained, the company employs its own mechanic.

Now well into its fifth successful decade, the company is mainly run by son Alan and daughter Caroline; another son, Robert, is living in Australia. Caroline looks after one of the depots, and Alan's wife Dawn is in charge of stock control. This gives owners John and Joan time to pursue their other interests - local people will know that John has been a director of Coventry City Football Club for the last 15 years, and may also be aware that he is a fine local artist, with one of his pictures recently fetching several hundred pounds at a recent charity auction . . . just one more reason why Coventry is fortunate to have this multi-talented family in its community!

Above: *Alan Reason with one of today's lorries.*
Below: *Part of the fleet today outside the premises in Binley Industrial Estate.*

Quality on wheels

For fifty years, The Park Sheet Metal Company has been concentrating on quality. Established in 1948 by partners George Payne, Stan Taylor and Nobby Clark, the company set out to produce high quality sheet metal components for all industries but primarily for the automotive industry. The three

founders were themselves all fully-skilled and experienced sheet metal workers. Having found suitable premises for their new venture in Holbrook Lane, their next task was to decide on a name for their new company; and as the premises happened to be opposite Parkgate, it seemed logical to call it The Park Sheet Metal Company.

The company quickly became renowned for the excellence of its craftsmanship and its products, and soon established links with Britain's most prestigious motor manufacturers, including Alvis, Armstrong Siddeley, Daimler and Rolls Royce. Within two years, George Payne had bought his partners out and taken sole charge of the growing firm. He moved to the firm's present site on Bayton Road in 1955, subsequently

expanding in the late 1960s to a site on Blackhorse Road, and some ten years later occupying a further unit on the Bayton Road Industrial Estate. The Suez crisis made the late 1950s a difficult time for the motor industry, and as the crisis escalated the industry was brought to a virtual standstill. Park Sheet Metal Company survived and consolidated its position by becoming, in 1958, an associate company of Motor Panels (Coventry) Limited. This association has enabled Park Sheet Metal Company to continue operating in its own niche market, specialising in low-volume, handmade sheet metal work for luxury car bodies and one-off prototypes, while Motor Panels (Coventry) Limited concentrates on high-volume production.

For any company which professes to set world-class standards, the skills of its workforce are paramount. Park Metal Company has, from the very beginning, been a

Top left: *George Payne, one of the co-founders of the firm.*
Right: *Alvis Graber front ends.*
Below: *Daimler Majestic Major limousines being manufactured in the 1950s.*

for niche markets. The company has carried out prestige programmes for leading car manufacturers including Daimler, Ford, Jaguar, Rolls-Royce and Rover. Interesting projects over the years have varied from the construction of Daimler Majestic Major limousines in the late 1950s, to the manufacture of the body for the Rolls Royce Camargue, the last of which was made in the late 1980s. More recently the Company was responsible for the construction of the Jaguar XJ220 prototype.

The running of this prestigious family company has now passed down to George Payne's son Tim. Tim, as Managing Director, is assisted by his brother Jonathon who is a Director, and the third generation of the founder's family has now become involved, with Stephen and Richard, Tim's sons, and Andrew who is Jonathon's son, all learning the business.

leader in skill training for sheet metal work. A staff of over 150 are currently employed, of whom over 80 are skilled sheet metal workers. Nowadays, of course, the company's exceptionally high levels of traditional craft skills are supplemented by equally advanced design skills using the latest computer equipment within a modern simultaneous engineering environment. The Company has developed specialised techniques for CAD interface, CMM measurement, CNC manufacturing equipment, and also, very importantly, the development of low-cost tooling and jig design and manufacture. Project management is becoming a vitally important aspect of the business, and all programme aspects are controlled through formalised cost-accountable project management systems. The company is thus able to meet its customers' exacting criteria, with ever-increasing emphasis on very short lead times, rapid response and low investment costs.

The Park Sheet Metal Company's proprietors and workforce alike can be proud of having spent 50 years, to date, at the forefront of their industry. It is the combination of their skill, craftsmanship, advanced technology and sound management which has created many world-beating, prestige products, and brought especial pleasure to all those who appreciate truly great motor cars.

Top left: The last Camargue body made for Rolls Royce, 24th May 1985. Above: The original prototype for the Jaguar XJ220. Below: An aerial view of the Blackhorse Road site in the late 1980s.

Providing a genuine full service capability, the Company carries projects from prototype creation and modification right through to production, where special processes adapted to low volume manufacture are employed. The Park Sheet Metal Company is a leader in the development of prototyping techniques, where it adheres to world class quality standards, and also provides a service to vehicle manufacturers and others giving informed advice on all sheet metal materials and their applications.

With clients in engineering, construction and domestic appliances, the company's activities are by no means restricted solely to the automotive industry; but it is the motor industry which offers the most scope with its continual requirements for prototypes, concept vehicles and modified vehicles

Making a mucky business clean and green

Some of the processes carried out by Exhall Plating Limited on the Bayton Road Industrial Estate sound incomprehensible to the uninitiated; one can begin to understand Barrel Zinc Plating, and perhaps even Manganese Phosphate, but what does one make of Vibratory De-Burring? Or Pickle & Oil?

But whatever these processes involve, one thing is certain: if it is done by Exhall Plating, it is done cleanly and with the utmost care and respect for the environment. The metal-finishing industry might not be the most obvious candidate for environmental awards, but Exhall Plating is collecting them, having been named Environmentalist of the Year at the 1998 Manufacturing Industry Achievement Awards, named as Finisher of the Year for 1998 by their trade body the Metal Finishing Association and won the BT sponsored Evening Telegraph Care for the Environment Award in 1997 - to name but a few of their achievements.

Exhall Plating is a family-run business. Started in 1952 by ex-RAF Harry Whomersley, its original site was in School Lane, Exhall; these premises have since been demolished and replaced by private

housing. In 1955 the business moved to the Foleshill Road, where it remained for some fifteen years; its next move brought it to the Bayton Road Industrial Estate, where it has expanded, currently occupying five units along the same road. The current Managing Director is Peter Starley, Harry Whomersley's son-in-law, and it is Peter's passionate commitment to protecting the environment which has earned the firm the respect of environmental campaigners.

The surface finishing of metals gives added value to the manufacturers components in the form of corrosion resistance and cosmetic appearance and is carried

Top: The sorting and packing department at Brindley Road. Left: Peter Starley and Mark McGuire (Environmental Manager) with Finisher of the Year and the Environmental Awards from the Metal Finishers Association.

effluent concentration well within water authority limits; and storage of materials is now carefully managed. A full-time environmental manager is employed, and overall some £1 million has been invested in the scheme. The Company's original aim of accreditation to an environmental standard in recognition of its environmental excellence was soon achieved; in fact, Exhall Plating was the first company in the United Kingdom to obtain simultaneous accreditation to both International and European environmental standards, ISO 14001 and EMAS (Eco-Management and Audit Scheme), and also holds BS EN ISO 9002.

As an added bonus, economic benefits to the Company have resulted, partly from its increased energy efficiency and partly from increased sales to customers who are themselves environmentally-aware and prefer to deal with firms who share their commitment. Another benefit which Exhall offers to customers is an innovative one-stop service at its new state-of-the-art sorting and packing facility at Brindley Road South, where a PACE optical sorting machine checks the manufacturing characteristics of customer's components and automatically rejects any found to have a defect. This facility is an outcome of Exhall's schedule of constant reinvestment to ensure that they remain at the forefront of this competitive industry; providing secure employment for some 65 workers, this family-run company has succeeded not only in occupying a unique position amongst the very best metal finishers but in earning the respect of environmentalists beyond the industry.

out by Exhall Plating primarily for the automotive industry in the Midlands but also covers the electronics and agricultural industries amongst others. Electro-plating used to be seen as "a mucky business", and the various finishing processes at Exhall involve substances such as cyanide, phosphate and mineral oils, which can have potentially disastrous effects on the environment if not handled correctly. This fact was pointed out to Peter Starley in no uncertain terms by his children, Jim aged six and Cassie aged seven, one day in 1995 when they came home after doing an environmental project at school, and told their Dad that he was a polluter. Prompted by this to take a closer look at his company's procedures, Peter realised that there was indeed room for improvement, and approached Coventry environmental consultant Pró Enviro Limited for guidance in establishing an environmental management system.

As well as the issues of storage and disposal of hazardous substances and controlling effluent discharges, the high levels of energy and water consumption were highlighted by the initial environmental review as problem areas. Rather than tackle each issue in isolation, the Company took a far-sighted, holistic approach, with environmental protection as its central objective. Staff were given environmental awareness training, and the Company implemented a stringent reappraisal of all its activities preparatory to working out and implementing a formal management scheme based on minimising waste, recycling, monitoring usage of raw materials and energy, and converting to non-hazardous materials where possible.

As a result of this strategy, water consumption was reduced by 21 per cent in the first year; energy consumption was reduced by 13 per cent through process changes and monitoring; an effluent treatment plant has been put in to keep

Above: One of the 10 automatic plating lines at Exhall Plating. Below: Peter Starley receiving the Environmentalist of the Year Award from Angela Rippon and Simon Bright in 1998.

You want it? - They've got it!

Even today, moving from Sussex to Coventry is a big step to take. In 1915, such a move was a major upheaval, and when Mr H E Phillips, of Lewes, Sussex, took a lease on a small one-roomed shop at 93 King Street, Coventry, the arrival of a Sussex family amidst the close-knit Hillfields community must have aroused much curiosity.

Mr Phillips took over the former Williams Hardware Co on September 29th, and his wife and thirteen year old son joined him in the old-fashioned Victorian house the following month. To begin with, the new business mostly sold meat tins, frying pans, picture cord, gas mantles, fire bricks and blackout blinds; one of their best-selling lines during the first world war was wire netting, bought by local families who had resorted to keeping rabbits and hens 'for the pot'. However, having served a five years' apprenticeship with an ironmonger in Penrith, Mr Phillips' intention was to develop the shop into a specialist ironmongers. His son, Patrick Cottingham Phillips, decided to follow in his father's footsteps and was apprenticed to an

ironmonger in Bedford, where he learned a lot about the trade and also met the girl who later became his wife. He returned to Coventry in 1923 and joined his father in the shop, and when his father died in a tragic accident three years later his mother, Edith Phillips, carried on the business with Patrick's assistance.

Patrick had a shrewd business head. On his first day at the ironmongery in Bedford, a customer had asked for a fish kettle and he managed to find a very old one priced at 14s 6d. Realising that this was far too cheap he altered the price to 44s 6d, thereby earning the instant respect of the manager. Under his guidance, the business pulled through the slump, and during the second world war his ingenuity in locating unusual items earned them many loyal customers. Patrick frequently set off early in the morning for Birmingham or the Black Country, or even Sheffield, and waited for the works to open so that he could bring the goods back to Coventry and deliver them to customers within the day, giving virtually a 12 hour service. One of the business' biggest drawbacks at this time was that, being a small shop and part of a row, there was no room to expand, and it was difficult to compete with large companies from such small premises.

*Top right: Mr Patrick Cottingham Phillips with the bench mark showing the height above sea level, 1960. **Left:** Mr Phillips and Mr Davies burying a Time Capsule in the foundations of their extension in the early 1970s.*

However, the shadow factories growing up around Coventry opened up a whole new market; their staff, new to Coventry, placed most of their orders by telephone, and Phillips' helpful and friendly service earned them a lot of business from these factories. Increasingly, customers found that they could get from Phillips goods that they had been unable to find elsewhere - stirrup pumps, hurricane lamps, pickaxes, small shovels for women to use, roofing felt in large quantities, hundreds of pairs of wellington boots, a constant supply of tea towels and all kinds of blackout fittings. Patrick's mother and wife used their own sewing machines to make yards of blackout curtain, while Patrick fitted the curtain rails. As the war continued Phillips found itself supplying equipment and hardware to factory canteens and large aerodrome construction projects nationwide.

In 1942 the firm became a limited liability company, with Patrick and his mother as co-directors. Since that time the company has seen tremendous expansion. It became a distributor for Calor Gas in 1952, and in 1959 the foundations were laid for a new building in King William Street. The new store opened in 1961, with four floors packed with hardware, tools and ironmongery of all types. Four years later the basement and ground floor were extended to double their original size, and four years after that the first floor and office sections were extended. Phase IV of the building development followed in 1975 with an extra bay for the tool floor andfurther extensions to the basement and ground floor. Improvements to the yard in 1978 provided covered storage, and the main yard was roofed over some five years later.

Patrick Cottingham Phillips died in 1992 at the age of 90, and many friends, trade acquaintances and representatives of Coventry City Council attended his funeral to mark their appreciation of his services to Coventry and the ironmongery trade. Under the directorship of Mr G Davies and Mrs D B Davies, the firm continues to give the same polite, personal service and the same impressive choice of goods which customers have come to rely on from H E Phillips Ltd, the Midlands' finest ironmongery store.

Above: *The certificate presented to Mr Phillips in 1972 making him an Honorary Life Member of the National Federation of Ironmongers.* ***Below:*** *Mr Phillips receiving his twelfth Rolls Royce in succession.*

A 1950s view from the upper storey of the city arcade

Acknowledgments

Coventry Libraries Local Studies

Karen Berry

James Slater

Thanks are also due to:

Andrew Mitchell who penned the editorial text,

Margaret Wakefield and Mike Kirke for their copywriting skills